August 26, 2007

Happy 1st Anniversary!

God Bless your marriage
now and forever

Marie & Ron

DR. JAMES & SHIRLEY
DOBSON

Night Light

A DEVOTIONAL FOR COUPLES

Multnomah Publishers® *Sisters, Oregon*

NIGHT LIGHT
published by Multnomah Publishers, Inc.

© 2000 by James Dobson, Inc.
International Standard Book Number: 1-57673-674-1

Cover design by Uttley/DouPonce DesignWorks
Cover photo by Junichi Endo/Photonica

Scripture quotations are from:
The Holy Bible, New International Version
© 1973, 1984 by International Bible Society,
used by permission of Zondervan Publishing House.

The Holy Bible, King James Version (KJV)

Multnomah is a trademark of Multnomah Publishers, Inc.
and is registered in the U.S. Patent and Trademark Office.
The colophon is a trademark of Multnomah Publishers, Inc.

For information:
MULTNOMAH PUBLISHERS, INC.
POST OFFICE BOX 1720
SISTERS, OREGON 97759

04 05 06 — 15 14 13

This book is dedicated affectionately to married couples around the world. May the Lord grant you loving and caring relationships that will endure to the final moment of your lives together. It is our prayer that this devotional will help you achieve that worthy objective. God's blessings to you all.

Jim and Shirley Dobson

CONTENTS

Acknowledgments 6

Introduction 7

1. True Love 11

2. Servants by Choice 21

3. Prayer Partners 31

4. Till Death Do Us Part 41

5. Can We Talk? 53

6. A Husband's Role 63

7. A Wife's Role 73

8. His Unfailing Presence 83

9. That Lovin' Feeling 93

10. The Gift of Sex 105

11. How Trust Happens 115

12. Honor Your Mate 127

13. Choose Joy 137

14. The Money Game 149

15. The Power of Encouragement 161

16. To Fight or Not to Fight? 171

17. Will You Forgive Me? 183

18. You Are a Treasure 195

19. A Generous Spirit 207

20. Seeing with God's Eyes 219

21. "And Then We Had Kids" 229

22. The Divorce "Solution" 241

23. A Time to Laugh 253

24. Hold on to Hope 265

25. Dare to Grow 277

26. Glimpse the Moment 287

Epilogue 299

Notes 301

ACKNOWLEDGMENTS

Appreciation is expressed to our editor James Lund; to his editorial support team of Keith Wall, Judith St. Pierre, and David Kopp; to publisher Don Jacobson; and to our other friends at Multnomah who helped us with this book. Thanks to each of you. Writing *Night Light* has been a very enjoyable experience.

*O*n a warm August night in Pasadena, California, a twenty-four-year-old man dressed in a black and white tuxedo and a twenty-three-year-old woman wearing a resplendent gown stood in a church and solemnly pledged their undying love to each other. The young man slipped a silver band on the woman's finger, wishing he could have afforded a diamond ring. Then the couple knelt at the altar as the minister (the groom's father) prayed this beautiful prayer of dedication:

> O eternal God: We bring Thee our children, Jimmy and Shirley. They were Thine, but Thou in love didst lend them to us for a little season to care for, to love, and to cherish. It has been a labor of love that has seemed but a few days because of the affection we bear them. Fresh from Thy hand they were in the morning of their lives. Clean and upright, but yet two separate personalities. Tonight we give them back to Thee—no longer as two—but as one flesh. *May nothing short of death dissolve the union here cemented.* And to this end let the marvelous grace of God do its perfect work!
>
> It is also our earnest prayer for them, *not* that God shall have a part in their lives, but that He shall have the preeminent part; not that they shall possess faith, but that faith shall fully possess them both; that in a materialistic world they shall not live for the earthly and temporal alone, but that they shall be enabled to lay hold of that which is *spiritual* and *eternal.*
>
> Let their lives together be like the course of the sun—rising in strength, going forth in power, and shining more and more unto the perfect day. Let the end of their lives resemble the setting of the sun—going down in a sea of glory, only to shine on

undimmed in the firmament of a better world than this.

In the name of the Father, and of the Son, and of the Holy Ghost. Amen.

Many in attendance that night had moist eyes by the time the minister had finished his prayer. Then he pronounced the couple "man and wife" and said with a wry smile, "Kiss 'er Jim." The groom didn't argue. After greeting the well-wishers, eating some dreadful cake, and posing for the perspiring photographer, they left on a low-budget honeymoon. And...they had only just begun.

How quickly the years have flown since that humble beginning more than four decades ago. Marriage has fulfilled all their youthful expectations and dreams. The man and woman are still deeply committed to each other and have enjoyed the sweet benefits of a happy, successful, loving relationship. Every good and perfect gift has been showered upon them, including the blessing of two great kids, who are now grown and serving the Lord in their communities.

Of course, the journey has not been without stresses and difficulties. The man's beloved parents died much too soon, and an assortment of illnesses and challenges have visited the couple along the way. But there has not been one moment in these forty years when they have wished to be free or have regretted the decision they made in their youth.

As you may have guessed by this point, we are the fortunate couple—Jim and Shirley Dobson. Our purpose in preparing this devotional has been to share some of the experiences and concepts that have strengthened our marriage through the years, in the hope that what we have learned will benefit those who are younger.

We are deeply concerned about the scourge of divorce that plagues mankind today. A recent study conducted at Rutgers University concluded that the institution of marriage appears to be dying in the United States. Similar trends are occurring in nations around the world. Since 1960 cohabitation has increased by 1,000 percent, with millions of naive couples entering into nonbinding, uncommitted relationships that are destined to flame out. Boredom and disenchantment, or both, are virtually inevitable after a few years. By the time they go their separate ways, the man and woman may have a child or two—children who will never enjoy the security of a stable, dedicated, two-parent family. It is a very sad sign of the times.

Why do young couples do it? Why do they settle for impermanent, unsatisfying, counterfeit relationships instead of committing themselves to lifelong love? We believe it is because many have a pervasive fear of marriage. They have watched their mothers and fathers claw each other to pieces. Teens and young adults want desperately to find someone to love but are afraid of being vulnerable—of being rejected and abandoned. Some wonder if marriage itself is passé and whether lifelong love is still achievable in today's world.

Well, we are living testimony to the fact that marriage based on a foundation of biblical principles is not only still workable, but offers the most fulfilling human relationship possible. There is nothing quite like being loved unconditionally and intimately, decade after decade, by someone who promises to be there for better or worse, in sickness and health, whether richer or poorer, forsaking all others—*all* others—until separated by death. It is a plan that bears the wisdom and compassion of the Creator Himself. The three pillars on which such a relationship is based are a deep and unshakable faith in Jesus Christ, an ironclad commitment to each other, and a dependence upon the eternal truths of the Holy Scriptures. With those weapons in the family arsenal, nothing can tear down the fortress of love.

Night Light is designed to help you build on such a foundation. It provides twenty-six weeks (six months) of devotionals that explore different topics relating to marriage: communication, romance, forgiveness, money, humor, and many more. Each Sunday an inspirational story, followed by a brief commentary, introduces a different theme. The sessions planned for Monday through Friday address the theme through Scripture verses, insights, suggestions, and a few provocative questions to encourage deeper intimacy between you, your spouse, and the Lord. A prayer concludes the day. Then Shirley gets the last word on Saturday, when she wraps up the week with a final comment.

9

A key feature of *Night Light* is that it is intended for couples to read *together*. We know that you are busy and under stress. We understand that you often approach the end of the day with barely enough energy to brush your teeth, let alone think about analyzing every facet of your marriage. That's why we've designed each session to offer helpful information and insights in ten minutes or less. As you read the stories and commentaries, we hope you will reflect on the relevant passages of Scripture and consider how they apply to your family. There is hope, humor, and practical wisdom in the pages of this book. Our prayer is that our words will enrich your spiritual life, bring you closer to your partner, and renew your marriage.

May God bless you both. Happy reading...and don't forget to turn off the light.

Jim and Shirley Dobson

True Love

"SHMILY"

by Laura Jeanne Allen

My grandparents were married for over half a century. From the time they met each other they played their own special game. The goal of their game was to write the word "shmily" in a surprise place for the other to find. They took turns leaving "shmily" around the house, and as soon as one of them discovered it, it was his or her turn to hide it once more.

They dragged "shmily" with their fingers through the sugar and flour containers to await whoever was preparing the next meal. They smeared it in the dew on the windows overlooking the patio where my grandma always fed us warm, homemade pudding with blue food coloring. "Shmily" was written in the steam on the bathroom mirror, where it would reappear after every hot shower. At one point, my grandmother even unrolled an entire roll of toilet paper to leave "shmily" on the very last sheet.

There was no end to the places "shmily" popped up. Little notes with a hastily scribbled "shmily" were found on dashboards and car seats or taped to steering wheels. The notes were stuffed inside shoes and left under pillows. "Shmily" was written in the dust upon the mantel and traced in the ashes of the fireplace. This mysterious word was as much a part of my grandparents' house as the furniture.

It took me a long time before I fully appreciated my grandparents' game. Skepticism has kept me from believing in true love—one that is pure and enduring. However, I never doubted my grandparents' relationship. They had love down pat. It was more than their flirtatious little games; it was a way of life. Their relationship was based on a devotion and passionate affection that not everyone experiences.

Grandma and Grandpa held hands every chance they could. They stole kisses as they bumped into each other in their tiny kitchen. They finished each other's sentences and shared the daily crossword puzzle and word jumble. My grandma whispered to me about how cute my grandpa was, how handsome an old man he had grown to be. She claimed that she really knew "how to pick 'em." Before every meal they bowed their heads and gave thanks, marveling at their blessings: a wonderful family, good fortune, and each other.

But there was a dark cloud in my grandparents' life: My grandmother had breast cancer. The disease had first appeared ten years earlier. As always, Grandpa was with her every step of the way. He comforted her in their yellow room, painted that way so that she could always be surrounded by sunshine, even when she was too sick to go outside.

Now the cancer was again attacking her body. With the help of a cane and my grandfather's steady hand, she went to church with him every Sunday. But my grandmother grew steadily weaker until, finally, she could not leave the house anymore. For a while, Grandpa would go to church alone, praying to God to watch over his wife. Then one day, what we all dreaded finally happened. Grandma was gone.

"Shmily." It was scrawled in yellow on the pink ribbons of my grandmother's funeral bouquet. As the crowd thinned and the last mourners turned to leave, my aunts, uncles, cousins, and other family members came forward and gathered around Grandma one last time. Grandpa stepped up to my grandmother's casket and, taking a shaky breath, began to sing to her. Through his tears and grief, the song came, a deep and throaty lullaby.

Shaking with my own sorrow, I will never forget that moment. For I knew that, although I couldn't begin to fathom the depth of their love, I had been privileged to witness its unmatched beauty.

S-h-m-i-l-y: See How Much I Love You.

Thank you, Grandma and Grandpa, for letting me see.

Is there any doubt that this tender couple knew the joy that springs from true love? That they understood the meaning of intimacy and commitment in marriage? Through a simple message sent in simple ways—traced in a flour container or on the bathroom mirror—this husband and wife continually expressed their love to each other for over fifty years. And when the time came for "Grandpa" to face the world alone, through his tears he sang his bride a lullaby that told her one last time, "See how much I love you!"

So many couples today reach the end of their days without ever experiencing such genuine love—the kind that includes stealing kisses, finishing each other's sentences, and holding hands whenever possible. They sincerely desire a deep, intimate love, but they assume it will just "happen" somewhere along the way. When it doesn't, disillusionment and even divorce follow.

We'll talk this week about true love—what it means and how you can achieve it in marriage. I'll close tonight's reading with this question: What does true love mean to you?

JCD

LOVE AT FIRST SIGHT

Love is of God.
1 John 4:7

*S*ome people believe that true love can occur the moment a man and woman lay eyes on each other. But "love at first sight" is a physical and emotional impossibility because you cannot love someone you don't even know. You have simply been drawn to the package in which they live.

A lifelong emotional attachment is much more than a romantic feeling. It is more than a sexual attraction or the thrill of the chase or a desire to get married. Such feelings usually indicate infatuation and tend to be temporary and rather selfish in nature. A person may say, "I can't believe what is happening to me. This is the most fantastic thing I've ever experienced! I must be in love." Notice that those who make these statements are not talking about the other person—they're excited about their own gratification. Such individuals haven't fallen in love with someone else; they've fallen in love with love.

Genuine love is not something one "falls" into, as though he or she was tumbling into a ditch. One cannot love an unknown object, regardless of how beautiful or handsome it is. Only when a person begins to develop a deep appreciation and admiration for another—an intense awareness of his or her needs, strength, and character—has one begun to experience true love. From there, it should grow for a lifetime.

Just between us...

- Do you remember thinking that you were in love as a teenager, only to have that feeling fade over time?
- What did you think and feel when we first met?
- How did God show you that I should be your marriage partner?

Dear Heavenly Father, thank You for the wonderful gift of love. Grant us your blessings, Father—more than we can even imagine right now! Amen.

"THEN YOU CAME"

Love never fails.
1 Corinthians 13:8

*T*he young husband was desperate. His wife had abandoned him and their two children weeks before. Though she still called occasionally, he had no idea where she was. On the phone, he pleaded with her to come home and told her how much he and the children loved her, yet she continually rebuffed him. Was it time to give up and move on?

No. The husband used his meager savings to hire a detective, who found his wife living in a third-rate hotel across the country. The husband borrowed money for a plane ticket. Soon he was on her doorstep saying, "We love you so much. Won't you come home?" She fell apart in his arms, and they went home together.

Weeks later he asked why she hadn't come when he expressed his love repeatedly on the phone. "Because," she answered, "those were only words before. But then you came."

True love is more than words. It may involve flying across the country, even when it costs you your last nickel, to bring your spouse home.

Just between us...

- How have I shown you my love this week?
- If "actions speak louder than words," are my deeds shouting or whispering my love for you?
- What can I do this week to show my love for you?
- How, specifically, did Jesus show us His love?

Dear Lord Jesus, we want both our words and our actions to say "love" in personal, powerful, and positive ways. Show us new ways to "honor one another above ourselves." Amen.

HAPPILY EVER AFTER?

Are you married? Do not seek a divorce.
1 Corinthians 7:27

hat you have observed by looking around your social circles is born out by the numbers: According to nearly every relevant statistic, the institution of marriage is in serious trouble. The Council on Families in America reports that half of first marriages are likely to end in divorce. The National Center for Health Statistics tells us that the number of Americans choosing to marry is declining. And Brent Barlow, professor of family sciences at Brigham Young University, says that if cohabitation and divorce trends continue, "married" could become a minority status within ten years.

Obviously, millions of couples who were once deeply in love and believed they were wonderfully suited for each other are seeing their marriages fall apart. If you and your spouse are going to beat the odds, you will need to bring dedication and hard work to your relationship.

Does this challenge seem more like a threat than a promise? We have good news. First, couples who are willing to invest in their relationship will find the greatest fulfillment and meaning that life has to offer. That is the promise of a godly marriage. Statistics bear this fact out too! Second, you need not try to beat the odds alone. In fact, you were never meant to. But more on that tomorrow....

Just between us...

- What, specifically, does having a "happy marriage" mean to you?
- Are you happy? Why or why not?
- What can I do to bring more happiness to your life?

Heavenly Father, You designed the covenant of marriage from the beginning, and our marriage belongs to You. So bless our union with Your best! Draw us together, and draw us to You. Amen.

THE THIRD PARTY

*No one can lay any foundation other than
the one already laid, which is Jesus Christ.*
1 Corinthians 3:11

To experience genuine love with our mate, we must bring a third party into the equation—Jesus Christ. Only through this spiritual connection with Him can we begin to fulfill all the potential of the relationship we call marriage.

Anyone who studies the Bible will recognize numerous principles woven throughout that apply to married life. Judeo-Christian values have effectively guided men and women from the beginning. These values were inspired by the Creator Himself, the originator of the institution of marriage. No matter what society says, or how laws change, the precepts that make up this scriptural system remain *the* way to find love and happiness in life.

Establishing a personal relationship with Jesus Christ is the critical first step toward attaining every meaningful goal, including the intimacy we all seek. If you haven't already given your heart to Him, we urge you to do so. It will bring meaning and purpose to every dimension of your life—including your marriage. Tomorrow we'll explain how.

Just between us...

- How have we been putting biblical principles to work in our marriage?
- How can I encourage you to spend more time in God's Word?
- Have we both personally invited Jesus Christ to be Lord of our lives and of our marriage? If not, can we take that life-changing step right now?

Lord Jesus, You are the foundation of our marriage. Help us look to You and Your strength in every way as we build a life together. Amen.

THE MOMENT LIFE BEGINS

If anyone is in Christ, he is a new creation;
the old has gone, the new has come!
2 Corinthians 5:17

*I*f you and your mate genuinely want to experience true love—the kind that lasts throughout eternity—you must face the truth about your standing before God. According to the Bible, we are all born with a sinful nature (Romans 3:23). This sin problem prevents us from living God's way, whether as individuals or as a married couple. In fact, unresolved sin will block even your best efforts to have a successful marriage, because the inescapable outcome of sin is slavery to our worst impulses and—eventually—death (Romans 6:23).

But there is a wonderful alternative! Jesus Christ paid the price for your sin through His death on the cross. And through His miraculous resurrection, He rescued you from eternal destruction. You can reach out in faith to receive your free gift of new life. Jesus put the Good News this way: "For God so loved the world that he gave his one and only Son, that whoever believes in him shall not perish but have eternal life" (John 3:16).

It really is that simple: If you choose to repent of your sin and receive the gift of salvation through faith in Jesus Christ, you *will* be forgiven and receive His gift of eternal life.

If you do not know Jesus Christ in this intimate way, we invite you to offer the following prayer tonight. For every human being who invites Jesus into his or her heart, that is the moment real life begins!

Just between us...

- Have each of us made a choice to receive God's gift of salvation?
- If not, what is keeping us from making that choice?

God, I am a sinner in need of You. I can't live right or hope for eternal life on my own. Please forgive my sins. I believe that Jesus Christ is Your only Son. You sent Him to die in my place and set me free from sin. Thank You! Amen.

I LOVE YOU!

"This is my command: Love each other."
John 15:17

Onc of the best ways to sustain true love between you and your mate is to build a bridge of loving memories. I am reminded of a husband named Jim who was tragically killed in an accident while driving home from work. It was his wife Carol's fiftieth birthday. Rescue teams found two plane tickets to Hawaii in his pocket; he had planned to surprise Carol with them.

Months later, Carol was asked how she was coping. She answered that on their wedding day, she and Jim had promised to say "I love you" before noon each day of their marriage. Over the years it had become a fun—and often difficult—challenge. She recalled running down the driveway saying "I love you," even though she was angry at Jim. On other occasions she drove to his office to drop a note in his car before the noon deadline. The effort it took to keep that promise led to many positive memories of their years together.

The morning Jim died, he left a birthday card in the kitchen, then slipped out to the car. Carol heard the engine starting and raced outside. She banged on the car window until he rolled it down, then yelled over the roar of the engine, "Here on my fiftieth birthday, Mr. James E. Garret, I, Carol Garret, want to go on record as saying 'I love you!'"

"That's how I've survived," Carol said later. "Knowing that the last words I said to Jim were *I love you!*"

We can build bridges across the span of our lives in many ways—with cards and flowers, through special shared moments, or, like Jim and Carol, with a simple "I love you" expressed each day. Cherished memories established over the course of your marriage will give you and your mate the foundation for a genuine love that endures a lifetime.

SMD

Servants by Choice

I'M THIRD

from the Denver Post

*O*ut of the sun, packed in a diamond formation and flying as one that day, the Minute Men dove at nearly the speed of sound toward a tiny emerald patch on Ohio's unwrinkled crazy quilt below. It was a little after nine on the morning of June 7, 1958, and the destination of the Air National Guard's jet precision team was the famed Wright-Patterson Air Force Base, just outside Dayton.

On the ground, thousands of faces looked upward as Colonel Walt Williams, leader of the Denver-based Sabrejet team, gauged a high-speed pullout. For the Minute Men pilots—Colonel Williams, Captain Bob Cherry, Lieutenant Bob Odle, Captain John Ferrier, and Major Win Coomer—the maneuver was routine, for they had given their show hundreds of times before millions of people.

Low across the fresh, green grass the jet stream streaked, far ahead of the noise of the planes' own screaming engines. Judging his pull-up, Colonel Williams pressed the microphone button on top of his throttle: "Smoke on—now!" The diamond of planes pulled straight up into the turquoise sky, a bush tail of white smoke pluming out behind. The crowd gasped as the four ships suddenly split apart, rolling to the four points of the compass and leaving a beautiful, smoky fleur-de-lis inscribed on the heavens. This was the Minute Men's famed "flower burst" maneuver. For a minute the crowd relaxed, gazing at the tranquil beauty of the huge, white flower that had grown from the lush Ohio grasslands to fill the great bowl of sky.

Out on the end of his stem of the flower, Colonel Williams turned his Sabre hard, cut off the smoke trail, and dropped the nose of his F86 to pick up speed for the low-altitude crossover maneuver. Then, glancing back over his shoulder, he froze in terror. Far across the sky to the east, John Ferrier's plane was rolling. He was in trouble. And his plane was headed right for the small town of Fairborn, on the edge of Patterson Field. In a moment, the lovely morning had turned to horror. Everyone saw; everyone understood. One of the planes was out of control.

Steering his jet in the direction of the crippled plane to race after it, Williams radioed urgently, "Bail out, John! Get out of there!" Ferrier still had plenty of time and room to eject safely. Twice more Williams issued the command: "Bail out, Johnny! Bail out!"

Each time, Williams was answered only by a blip of smoke.

He understood immediately. John Ferrier couldn't reach the mike button on the throttle because both hands were tugging on a control stick locked in full-throw right. But the smoke button was on the stick, so he was answering the only way he could—squeezing it to tell Walt he thought he could keep his plane under enough control to avoid crashing into the houses of Fairborn.

Suddenly, a terrible explosion shook the earth. Then came a haunting silence. Walt Williams continued to call through the radio, "Johnny? Are you there? Captain, answer me!"

No response.

Major Win Coomer, who had flown with Ferrier for years, both in the Air National Guard and with United Airlines, and who had served a combat tour with him in Korea, was the first Minute Man to land. He raced to the crash scene, hoping to find his friend alive.

Instead, he found a neighborhood in shock from the awful thing that had happened. Captain John T. Ferrier's Sabrejet had hit the ground midway between four houses, in a backyard garden. It was the only place where he could have crashed without killing people. The explosion had knocked a woman and several children to the ground, but no one had been hurt, with the exception of Johnny Ferrier. He had been killed instantly.

A steady stream of people began coming to Coomer as he stood in his flying suit beside the smoking, gaping hole in the ground where his best friend had just died.

"A bunch of us were standing together, watching the show," an elderly man with tears in his eyes told Coomer. "When the pilot started to roll, he was headed straight for us. For a second, we looked right at each other. Then he pulled up right over us and put it in there."

In deep humility, the old man whispered, "This man died for us."

LOOKING AHEAD...

A few days after this tragic accident, John Ferrier's wife, Tulle, found a worn card in his billfold. On it were the words "I'm Third." That simple phrase exemplified the life—and death—of this courageous man. For him, God came first, others second, and himself third.

True to his philosophy, John Ferrier sacrificed his life for people he had never met. If you ever found yourself in a similar situation, would you do the same? In the coming week we're going to ask how one develops the attitude of a servant.

JCD

DOING WHAT COMES NATURALLY

Surely I was sinful at birth, sinful from
the time my mother conceived me.
Psalm 51:5

*H*umanistic and Christian psychologists differ significantly in how they view human nature. Secular psychologists see children as born "good," or at least "morally neutral." They believe children learn to do wrong from parental mistakes and a corrupt society.

As Christians, however, we know otherwise. Deep within our character is a self-will that is inborn, part of our genetic nature. We desire to control people, our circumstances, our environment—we want what we want, and we want it now. Adam and Eve demonstrated this when they ate the forbidden fruit. Toddlers stamp their little feet and throw temper tantrums. Husbands and wives illustrate the same willfulness when they argue about how to spend money—or about whether the toilet paper should roll from the front or the back. King David referred to this basic human nature when he wrote, "In sin did my mother conceive me."

Only Jesus Christ can help us deal with the depravity that leads us to be selfish, arrogant, and disobedient. He has promised to do for us what we are powerless to accomplish on our own. Let's talk about that.

Just between us...

- Do you agree that humans are born with a bent toward sin? Why or why not?
- Is there an area of your life that used to be a struggle, but that you've given over to God with positive results?
- Do you think selfishness is a problem in our marriage?
- How can we encourage each other in this area?

Father, we admit our sinful and selfish ways. We look to You for forgiveness and healing. Thank You for Your mercies. We need Your power to change—and we reach for it together. Amen.

I DESERVE IT!

For the sinful nature desires what is contrary to the Spirit,
and the Spirit what is contrary to the sinful nature.
Galatians 5:17

That sinful nature we talked about yesterday often rears its head in the form of the thought *I deserve more.* It leads us to demand the best deal, the lion's share, the most credit, and the finest of everything. From earliest childhood, as we have seen, our impulse is to focus on ourselves and to disregard the needs of others.

And, yes, this "I-deserve-it" attitude can permeate marriages. Resentment can build over who works the hardest, who spends more than his or her share of the money, and who is not doing enough to serve the other. Anger then erupts over insignificant irritants that bubble up from the cauldron of emotions. Many fights in marriage begin with the belief that we're being cheated in the relationship.

Beware of this trap. The minute we begin thinking that we are entitled to more, we've started down the slippery road to selfishness. It can devastate a relationship.

John Ferrier didn't deserve to die in an Ohio neighborhood—but when crisis came, he chose to sacrifice for others. Jesus didn't deserve to be nailed to a wooden cross—but out of love for the Father and for us, He allowed Himself to be crucified. This kind of sacrificial love seeks to serve, not "deserve"—and that changes everything!

Just between us...

- What do you feel we truly deserve in this life?
- Do you sometimes feel that you're not getting what you deserve in our marriage?
- Is selfishness a problem for us?

Dear Lord, we need Your Spirit at work in us to overcome our self-centered impulses. By Your grace, empower us to serve instead of to "deserve." Amen.

LOVE BY SERVING

> *"Now that I, your Lord and Teacher, have washed*
> *your feet, you also should wash one another's feet."*
> John 13:14

*H*usband, we're speaking especially to you tonight. Just as selfishness is a sure marriage killer, an attitude of service and sacrifice—the "I'm Third" philosophy—is an indisputable marriage builder.

We urge you to study your wife. What is it that speaks to her heart? Are you providing that for her? Would she appreciate help with the dishes, vacuuming, or changing the baby's diaper? Should you be more romantic? Could you put off that weekend auto show so she can visit her sister? Maybe you'd rather go fishing on Saturday, but should you watch the kids instead so your wife can have a needed day out?

Jesus gave us a classic example of service when He washed His disciples' feet and told them to do the same for one another. Is it time for some symbolic "foot washing" in your marriage? Women are romantic creatures. God made them that way. Have you tried to understand that tender nature and sought to meet the needs it expresses?

Here's the personal payoff: If you as a husband will address this romantic longing, your wife, being a responder, will be drawn closer to you. You'll get the kind of attention and admiration you hope for. Try it!

Just between us...

- (husband) When have I done a good job of "foot washing" in our marriage?
- (husband) Do you feel I understand your romantic nature? Why or why not?
- (husband) Have I met your needs during the past week?

(husband) *Dear Lord, I want to become an expert at meeting my wife's needs. Teach me to "wash her feet" and serve my way to a great marriage. Amen.*

What a Man Needs

It is not good for the man to be alone.
I will make a helper suitable for him.
Genesis 2:18

ife, do you understand the needs of your husband? Let's face it, a man's career is usually extremely important to his self-esteem. He is made that way. Many women complain about their husbands' "workaholism," which may be valid, and yet husbands deserve thanks for the effort they invest. Compared to the man who sits around the house doing little or nothing, the hard worker is an honorable man. God has assigned two key tasks to men: to provide for and to protect their families. If your husband meets those two requirements, you need to let him know that you appreciate how hard he works.

Several years ago a survey was taken to determine what men wanted in their homes. The result was surprising: It was *tranquility*. Is your home a peaceful haven for your husband and your family—a place where he can "recharge his batteries" and enjoy the company of his family?

Whatever his specific needs and wants, your husband—and your marriage—will benefit immeasurably when you make him a priority in your life. Scripture says that a woman was designed to be a "helper" for her husband (who, in turn, is commanded to love his wife as Christ loved the church). And after all, there's no one better for the job than you.

Just between us...

- (wife) Do you feel that I appreciate how hard you work?
- (wife) What do I do for you that you most appreciate?
- (wife) What things could I do to show my love for you this week?

(wife) *Heavenly Father, thank You for my husband. I want to understand and serve him in ways that refresh and encourage him. Show me how to bless him with beautiful gifts like appreciation, support, and tranquility. Amen.*

DENY YOURSELF

> *"If anyone would come after me, he must deny*
> *himself and take up his cross and follow me."*
> Matthew 16:24

Television advertisers are experts at "rattling the cages" of viewers. They understand the philosophy of today's audience: Look out for number one. That's why we're bombarded with slogans such as "Have it your way"; "You deserve a break today"; and "Because I'm worth it." Their goal is to appeal to our self-centered nature and manipulate us into buying a product. Frequently, they succeed.

The "I'm Third" approach to life is in direct contradiction to the message of these ads. And well it should be! Jesus tells us that our first obligation in following Him must be to deny ourselves—to let go of the steering wheel, so to speak, and let the Lord drive. Secondly, we are to love and care for others. Try implementing these priorities. They will lead to a better marriage in this life and eternal rewards in the next.

God first, others second, myself third. A simple phrase, but it contains far more wisdom for living life to the fullest than anything you'll see or hear on a television ad.

Just between us...

* Do we have an "I'm Third" kind of marriage?
* Do we know a couple who model this philosophy?
* How do you feel about putting my desires ahead of your own?
* What, if anything, do we need to change to create an "I'm Third" marriage?
* How can we specifically ask God to help us make this happen?

Dear Jesus, we hear Your invitation to follow You in a life of self-denial. Tonight we make You Lord of our marriage. Help us to live every day by Your example—in obedience to the Father and in loving service to each other. Amen.

WILLING SACRIFICE

Love is patient, love is kind.... It is not self-seeking.
1 Corinthians 13:4–5

*N*othing does more for a marriage than the willing sacrifices made by one spouse for the other. I remember an example of this from early in our marriage. Jim and I were both teaching elementary school, and we often stayed up late during the week to grade papers. Then on the weekends, Jim spent long hours studying as he pursued his doctoral degree. I was a good sport about it, but it wasn't easy. All our friends were fixing up their homes, buying furniture, going out for dinner, taking vacations, and having children.

Shortly after Jim began his graduate work, he told me that he realized what a difficult time it was for me. He felt that his studies were beginning to interfere with our marriage and that, as he put it, "nothing is worth that price." He decided to postpone working on his degree so we could spend more time together. He took a very light load of classwork that semester so we could "reconnect" emotionally. I will always love and respect Jim for making that choice. He cared more about me than his personal ambition and career!

I'm sure that Tulle Ferrier, the wife of the doomed pilot, never forgot the sacrifices that must have been part of her marriage with her husband, John. I'm sure she didn't want to lose him in that terrible crash. But I also imagine that she must have loved and appreciated living with a man who had his priorities in order—God first, others second, and self third—and that she wouldn't have changed him for the world. That is, I believe, the essence of a successful marriage.

SMD

Prayer Partners

PROTECTED BY PRAYER

by Cheri Fuller

The missionary rose and prepared to leave the campsite where he had spent the night en route to the city for medical supplies. He extinguished his small campfire, pulled on his canvas backpack, and hopped on his motorcycle to continue his ride through the African jungle. Every two weeks he made this two-day journey to collect money from a bank and purchase medicine and supplies for the small field hospital where he served. When he completed those errands, he hopped on his bike again for the two-day return trip.

When the missionary arrived in the city, he collected his money and medical supplies and was just about to leave for home when he saw two men fighting in the street. Since one of the men was seriously injured, the missionary stopped, treated him for his injuries, and shared the love of Christ with him. Then the missionary began his two-day trek home, stopping in the jungle again to camp overnight.

Two weeks later, as was his custom, the missionary again made the journey to the city. As he ran his various errands, a young man approached him—the same man the missionary had ministered to during his previous trip. "I knew you carried money and medicine with you," the man said, "so my friends and I followed you to your campsite in the jungle after you helped me in the street. We planned to kill you and take all the money and drugs. But just as we were about to move in and attack you, we saw twenty-six armed guards surround and protect you."

"You must be mistaken," said the missionary. "I was all alone when I spent the night in the jungle. There were no guards or anyone else with me."

"But sir, I wasn't the only one who saw the guards. My five companions saw them, too. We counted them! There were twenty-six bodyguards, too many for us to handle. Their presence stopped us from killing you."

Months later, the missionary related this story to the congregation gathered at his home church in Michigan. As he spoke, one of the men listening stood up and interrupted him to ask the exact day the incident in the jungle had occurred. When the missionary identified the specific month and day of the week, the man told him "the rest of the story."

"On the exact night of your incident in Africa, it was morning here in Michigan, and I was on the golf course. I was about to putt when I felt a strong urge to pray for you. The urge was so strong that I left the golf course and called some men of our church right here in this sanctuary to join me in praying for you. Would all you men who prayed with me that day stand up?"

The missionary wasn't concerned with who the men were; he was too busy counting them, one by one. Finally he reached the last one. There were twenty-six men—the exact number of "armed guards" the thwarted attacker had seen.

LOOKING AHEAD...

Do you ever find yourself so caught up in the busyness of life that you forget about or postpone a time of prayer? I'm sure the missionary in the story above is one man who was grateful his congregation took seriously the urge to pray!

My father, James Dobson Sr., also took his prayer life seriously. He was known to spend hours at a time on his knees in conversation with the Lord. At Dad's request, the words "He Prayed" are written on the footstone of his grave. Through his example, and through God's response, I learned firsthand the power and privilege of prayer. In the week to come let's take a closer look at this awesome opportunity.

JCD

No Appointment Needed

*Evening, morning and noon I cry out
in distress, and he hears my voice.*
Psalm 55:17

*W*ould you ever visit your doctor unannounced and expect him to be available to see you? Can you imagine taking a spur-of-the-moment trip to the White House and immediately being ushered into the Oval Office to meet the president?

Of course you can't. You would need an appointment first—and a very good reason for being there! Yet, amazingly, you can "drop in" on someone far more important than the president of the United States. And you can expect that He will push aside all other business to talk with you.

Our heavenly Father yearns to have a personal, loving relationship with you. What an incredible concept that is! The King of the universe—the Creator of all heaven and earth, who has no needs and no shortcomings—cares about what we think and feel. That is almost incomprehensible. He wants to spend time with you, hear about your struggles and successes, encourage you, and share His glorious plans for you. Prayer is a wonderful privilege—a chance for direct communication with our Creator. No matter how busy He may be, He always has time in His schedule for you.

Just between us...

- What keeps us from praying more?
- Do you sometimes feel that the Lord is not listening when you pray?
- What specific prayer has the Lord answered for us over the years?
- How can we work toward a more vibrant prayer life together?

Heavenly Father, how grateful we are that we can talk to You! And how blessed we are that You listen and care! Thank You, loving Lord. Graciously receive even the longings in our hearts that find no words today. Amen.

To Hear Your Voice

Pray continually; give thanks in all circumstances,
for this is God's will for you in Christ Jesus.
1 Thessalonians 5:17–18

*W*ere you ever separated for an extended time from someone you loved deeply? If so, those days apart probably seemed almost unbearable. They may have also led to special moments to be savored—such as that catch-your-breath instant when you recognized the handwriting on the letter in your mailbox, realized who sent that last e-mail message, or heard that familiar voice over the telephone.

Jesus' love for us is something like that. He longs for fellowship with us. And when we kneel before Him and spend even a few minutes in prayer, we bring joy to Him. The apostle Paul said Jesus wants to hear your voice "continually" (1 Thessalonians 5:17). But, when we let ourselves get caught up in the busyness of life and put off time for prayer, we become less sensitive to His voice and His leading in our lives.

Relationships, whether human or divine, must be cultivated and maintained if they are to be vibrant and meaningful. Let's make sure we spend time every day with our loving Master.

Just between us...

- How do you feel when we're apart for several days?
- How can we make sure that no matter how busy we are, we keep talking to each other?
- Do you think we spend enough time with Jesus in prayer?
- How is it possible to pray "continually" amidst the busyness of our lives? Can we learn to be mindful of Him throughout the day?

Dear Lord, we seek a thriving prayer conversation with You. We need it—to know You better, to hear You more clearly, and to love each other more deeply. Teach us to pray. Amen.

THE POWER OF PRAYER

The prayer of a righteous man is powerful and effective.
James 5:16

I'll never forget the evening that Jim and I, exhausted after a long day, collapsed into bed without completing our usual practice of praying about many things, but especially for our children. We were almost asleep when I remembered.

"Jim," I said, "we haven't prayed for our kids yet today. Don't you think we should talk to the Lord?"

It wasn't easy, but we crawled out of bed, got on our knees, and offered yet another prayer for our children's well-being.

Later we learned that at the exact moment we were praying, a strange-looking man sought by the police tried to get into the parked car where our daughter, Danae, and a girlfriend were sharing a fast-food meal. By the grace of God, the door was locked, and Danae was able to start the car quickly and escape.

Never underestimate the power of prayer. When your petition is also for God's will, it will bring you closer to the heavenly Father, who loves you unconditionally.

Just between us...

- Can you share a personal example of the power of prayer?
- As a couple, do we usually rely on prayer and God's power, or do we usually try to solve our problems ourselves?
- Who among our friends and family needs prayer right now?
- How can I pray for you tonight?

Lord, thank You for the awesome power You make available to us through prayer. May all our requests honor You and help release Your best in our relationship. Amen.

THE FAMILY THAT PRAYS TOGETHER

For where two or three come together
in my name, there am I with them.
Matthew 18:20

The day you were married, you probably knelt together and shared a prayer during your wedding ceremony. In front of family and friends, you helped cement your union through this joint conversation with the Lord. Sadly, many couples never pray together again.

Don't misunderstand—prayer when you are alone, with a friend, in a Bible study, or in church is extremely important and valued just as much by our heavenly Father. But there is something special about prayer between husband, wife, and God that can't be found elsewhere. It creates a spiritual connection, accountability, and a holy bond that brings strength and stability to the relationship. It can even allow you to communicate about sensitive issues that might otherwise never come out—issues that can be discussed and prayed over in a spirit of humility and purity of motive.

The old saw "The family that prays together, stays together" still applies today. We encourage you to remember it the next time you kneel in prayer.

Just between us...

- When was our last meaningful prayer time together?
- What's the most common obstacle that keeps us from praying together?
- How do you feel about praying with me?
- How could we benefit from praying as a couple?
- Should we schedule a regular time of prayer together?

Father, You have blessed us with each other as partners in marriage. Show us how to make prayer—together—a regular part of our life. Amen.

FRIDAY

Manipulating Our Maker?

If we ask anything according to his will, he hears us.
1 John 5:14

*I*t's tempting for some of us to view our Lord as a heavenly "Mr. Fix-It"—a supernatural problem solver who can be manipulated according to our whims. We might make a little wager on our favorite football team and then pray for God to intervene so our team will win. Or on the day of the church picnic, we might pray for a rainstorm so we don't have to fix that potato salad we promised to bring.

Others see prayer as a negotiating tool. They want to make a deal with God: "Lord, if You give me this promotion at work...or allow me to get pregnant this month...or let that car at the dealership still be on sale...then I promise I'll do [fill in the blank] for You."

Of course these are foolish bargains that reveal a misunderstanding of the majesty of God. He is Lord of lords, King of kings, and Creator of all heaven and earth. He is not a deal maker who allows Himself to be manipulated. Instead, He wants us to carefully consider His will for our lives before we pray. Prayer is a privilege—a direct line to the Lord's eternal wisdom and love. Let's not forget what a blessing it is just to come into His presence.

Just between us...

- Have you ever tried to manipulate God through prayer?
- How can we be sure our prayer petitions are within God's will?
- Do our prayers include adoration, devotion, and intercession, or do they represent merely a daily "wish list"?
- How might our relationship change if we focused on prayer from God's perspective?

Heavenly Father, thank You for the privilege of bringing our requests to You. Give us a deep desire for Your will—not ours—for our marriage, and help us to shape our prayers and our priorities accordingly. Amen.

PERSISTENT PRAYER

They should always pray and not give up.
Luke 18:1

When I was only eight years old, I began praying for my dysfunctional family while alone in my bedroom. It still brings tears to my eyes to think that Jesus Christ was listening to me—a little child from a poor family—in those quiet moments. I had no status or influence in the community—no particular skills or talent that the Lord needed. And yet He accepted and blessed me in the years that followed. Those early prayers for a loving family, and later for a Christian husband, were answered beyond my greatest hopes and dreams.

Some of you reading this tonight, however, have also prayed unceasingly for what you believe is God's will—yet you've seen no evidence that He has even heard your prayers. I know of one husband and wife who have prayed for the salvation of their children for more than twenty-five years, with no hint of change. To those in a similar situation: I understand your discouragement. I don't know why the Lord chooses to grant some of our petitions more quickly than others—but I *do* know that He honors the prayers of His righteous followers, and that we should stay on our knees before Him.

Luke 18 records the parable Jesus told about the widow who approached a judge, day after day, asking for justice against her adversary. For some time the judge refused. Finally, however, he gave in, "so that she won't eventually wear me out with her coming!" Jesus was telling us to not give up, but to pray persistently for the desires of our hearts.

I have based my life on my belief in the power and importance of prayer. That's why I agreed to chair the National Day of Prayer Task Force. And it is why Jim and I have made prayer the cornerstone of our marriage. Consistent prayer can also undergird and sustain your marital relationship through the years. We encourage the two of you to bow before our great, loving God—tonight and every night.

SMD

Till Death Do Us Part

DO YOU WANT ME?

by Park York

I rise early on this Friday, as I do every day, to prepare coffee and mix a protein shake. The television news plays quietly in the corner. Flossie, my wife, is still asleep.

Sometime after eight, she begins floating out of slumber. I bring the shake to her bedside, put the straw in her mouth, and give her cheek a little pat as she begins to drink. Slowly the liquid recedes.

I sit there holding the glass, thinking about the past eight years. At first, she asked only an occasional incoherent or irrelevant question; otherwise she was normal. I tried for two years to find out what was wrong. She grew agitated, restless, defensive; she was constantly tired and unable to hold a conversation.

At last, a neurologist diagnosed Alzheimer's disease. He said he wasn't sure—a firm diagnosis could come only from examining brain tissue after death. There is no known cause for this malady. And no known cure.

I enrolled Flossie in a day care center for adults. But she kept wandering off the property. We medicated her to keep her calm. Perhaps from receiving too much of one drug, she suffered a violent seizure that left her immeasurably worse: lethargic, incontinent, and unable to speak clearly or care for herself. My anguish gradually became resignation. I gave up all plans of retirement travel, recreation, visits to see grandchildren—the golden era older people dream about.

The years have passed, and my days have become routine, demanding, lonely, seemingly without accomplishment to measure. Flossie has gradually dropped in strength and weight, from 125 pounds to 86. I take some time to work with a support group and to attend church, but the daily needs keep me feeding, bathing, diapering, changing beds, cleaning house, fixing meals, dressing and undressing her, and doing whatever else a nurse and homemaker does, morning to night.

Occasionally, a word bubbles up from the muddled processes of Flossie's diseased brain. Sometimes relevant, sometimes the name of a family member, or the name of an object. Just a single word.

On this Friday morning, after she finishes her shake, I give her some apple juice, then massage her arms and caress her forehead and cheeks. Most of the time her eyes are closed, but today she looks up at me, and suddenly her mouth forms four words in a row.

"Do you want me?"

Perfect enunciation, softly spoken. I want to jump for joy.

"Of course I want you, Flossie!" I say, hugging and kissing her.

And so, after months of total silence, she has put together the most sincere question a human being can ask. She speaks, in a way, for people everywhere: those shackled by sin, addiction, hunger, thirst, mental illness, physical pain—frightened, enervated people afraid of the answer, but desperate enough to frame the question anyway.

And, Flossie, I can answer you even more specifically. It may be difficult for you to understand what's happening. That's why I'm here, to minister God's love to you, to bring you wholeness, comfort, and release. Mine are the hands God uses to do His work, just as He uses others' hands in other places. In spite of our shortcomings, we strive to make people free, well, and happy, blessing them with hope for the future while bringing protein shakes every morning.

LOOKING AHEAD...

Unlike so many people today, this gentleman who so gently cared for his wife clearly understood the meaning of *commitment*. As her mind and body deteriorated with no hope for a cure, he willingly abandoned the hopes and dreams he had worked to achieve. She needed him desperately, and he would be there for her, even though she could give nothing back—not even a rational "thank you." This, in all its magnificence—and sorrow—is the meaning of love.

No doubt you have dreams of your own for the rest of your married life. Just remember that God may have other plans that depend on your unswerving commitment to each other—no matter what.

JCD

FOR BETTER AND WORSE?

For this reason a man will leave his father and mother and be
united to his wife, and they will become one flesh.

Genesis 2:24

*D*id you hear the one about the wedding ceremony of a young contract lawyer and his bride? When the minister got to the vows, he intoned, "Do you take this woman for better? For worse? For richer? For poorer? In sickness? And in health?"

He was startled to hear the groom cautiously reply, "Yes. No. Yes. No. No. And yes."

Of course, we'd all like to sign up for the better, richer, and healthier parts when we get married and forget all that other stuff. But that's not the way marriage works because that's not the way life works.

In another wedding ceremony, this one real, the bride and groom pledged to stay married as long as they *continued to love each other.* Let's hope they both know good divorce attorneys, because they're going to need them. Relationships based on feelings are necessarily ephemeral and transitory. The only real stability in marriage is produced by firm commitments that hold two people steady when emotions are fluctuating wildly. Without such determination, even the best relationship is destined to disintegrate.

Just between us...

- Are you still as committed to me as you were when we married?
- Are we prepared to "hang tough" when the going gets difficult?
- Why do you think so many couples don't stay together?
- What kind of commitment does the Lord expect of us?
- What can we do to make sure our commitment to marriage stays strong?

Dear God, in Your presence we renew our whole-hearted choice to love. Bless this holy commitment with courage, strength, tenacity—and most of all joy! Amen.

ROMAN BRIDGES

The winds blew and beat against that house;
yet it did not fall, because it had its foundation on the rock.
Matthew 7:25

*Y*esterday we talked about being committed to your partner for better and for worse. Another way to look at this issue was once related by the late Dr. Francis Schaeffer. He described the bridges that were built in Europe by the Romans in the first and second centuries A.D. The bridges still stand today, despite the unreinforced brick and mortar with which they were made, because they are used for nothing but foot traffic. If an eighteen-wheel semi were driven across those historic structures, they would crumble in a cloud of dust and debris.

Marriages that lack an iron-willed determination to hang together are like those Roman bridges. They appear to be secure and may indeed remain upright for many years—until they are put under heavy pressure. Then the supports split and the structure crumbles.

Is your marriage constructed to withstand unusual stress as well as normal wear? Take the time to install a proper foundation—the Lord Jesus Christ. Then build your relationship on habits and attitudes that will sustain it under heavy pressure.

Just between us...

- Has there ever been a time when our marriage seemed less than solid?
- Do we know a couple whose marriage has stayed secure under stress? What's their secret?
- Do we see any cracks—even tiny ones—beginning to appear in our marriage? What can we do to repair them?

Father, we turn to the unshakable truths of Your Word and the unfailing promise of Your presence to hold our marriage together. Thank You that we can live and love securely—even under stress—because You are in this marriage with us. Amen.

DOING THE RIGHT THING

*If anyone does not provide for his relatives, and
especially for his immediate family, he has denied the faith.*

1 Timothy 5:8

O ur friends Keith and Mary Korstjens have been married for more than forty years. Shortly after their honeymoon, Mary was stricken with polio and became quadriplegic. The doctors informed her that she would be confined to a wheelchair for the rest of her life. It was a devastating development, but Keith never wavered in his commitment to Mary. For all these years he has bathed and dressed her, carried her to and from her bed, taken her to the bathroom, brushed her teeth, and combed her hair.

Obviously, Keith could have divorced Mary in 1957 and looked for a new and healthier wife, but he never even considered it. We admire this man not only for doing the right thing, but for continuing to love and cherish his wife. Though the problems faced by the rest of us may be less challenging than those encountered by the Korstjens, each of us will confront some kind of hardship in the years ahead. How will we respond?

Just between us...

- Do you worry about failing health down the road?
- When you're sick, how well do I care for you?
- Have you ever resented having to serve me during times of sickness or disability?
- How could illness—either minor or serious—actually strengthen our marriage?

Lord, we don't want to deny the faith by failing to provide for those You have entrusted to our care. We ask for Your strength—especially when hardships come—to show enduring love in our marriage and in our family. Amen.

FRUSTRATING FOIBLES

Be kind and compassionate to each other,
forgiving each other, just as in Christ God forgave you.
Ephesians 4:32

*T*he great tragedies of life can undermine committed love, but so can minor frustrations. These daily irritants, when accumulated over time, may be even more threatening to a marriage than the catastrophic events that crash into our lives. And yes, there are times in every marriage when a husband and wife don't like each other very much. There may be occasions when anger or disappointment take the fun out of a relationship temporarily. Emotions are like that. They occasionally flatten out like an automobile tire with a nail in it. Riding on the rim is a pretty bumpy experience for everyone on board.

The next time you're tempted to trade in your spouse, remember that divorce must never be considered an option for those who are committed to each other for life. Instead, determine to work on your points of friction and to accept the human frailties and faults in your spouse. He or she must accept an equal number of flaws in you as well. A covenant of commitment and acceptance is a powerful secret to lifelong love.

Just between us...

* What "daily irritant" between us is most frustrating to you?
* Have we gotten better or worse at handling everyday aggravations?
* How can we reduce frustrations in our marriage?

Dear God, You know how little irritations often cause pain in our marriage. As we humbly release these irritations to You, please heal us. Forgive us our pride. Anoint us with grace. Grow in us a love that's stronger than any fault or foible. Amen.

"I PROMISE..."

"Simply let your 'Yes' be 'Yes,' and your 'No,' 'No.'"
Matthew 5:37

*L*ove can be defined in myriad ways, but in marriage "I love you" really means "I promise to be there for you all of my days." It is a promise that says, "I'll be there when you lose your job, your health, your parents, your looks, your confidence, your friends." It's a promise that tells your partner, "I'll build you up; I'll overlook your weaknesses; I'll forgive your mistakes; I'll put your needs above my own; I'll stick by you even when the going gets tough."

This kind of assurance will hold you steady through all of life's ups and downs, through all the "better or worse" conditions.

The Lord has demonstrated throughout the ages that He keeps His promises—including the most important one of all, reserving a spot in heaven for each of His followers, for all eternity. Since God keeps His promises, we must keep ours too—especially the one we made before God, our family, our friends, and our church on our wedding day.

Just between us...

- What part of my wedding vow means the most to you now?
- In what ways has our pledge to "stick together no matter what" seen us through hard times?
- How do we benefit spiritually from keeping our commitments?

Dear Lord, give us Your strength today to honor our promises. May our word be our bond—to each other, to our friends, and to family and associates. Thank You that You never waiver on Your promises to us! Amen.

A PERFECT AFFECTION

> *"What God has joined together,*
> *let man not separate."*
> Matthew 19:6

*I*n earlier generations most folks accepted without question the concept of marriage as a lifetime commitment. My father-in-law, James Dobson Sr., was no exception. This is what he said to his fiancée after she agreed to become his wife:

> I want you to understand and be fully aware of my feel-
> ings concerning the marriage covenant we are about to
> enter. I have been taught at my mother's knee, in har-
> mony with the Word of God, that the marriage vows
> are inviolable, and by entering into them I am binding
> myself absolutely and for life. The idea of estrangement
> from you through divorce for any reason at all
> [although God allows one—infidelity] will never at any
> time be permitted to enter into my thinking. I'm not
> naive in this. On the contrary, I'm fully aware of the
> possibility, unlikely as it now appears, that mutual
> incompatibility or other unforeseen circumstances
> could result in extreme mental suffering. If such
> becomes the case, I am resolved for my part to accept it
> as a consequence of the commitment I am now mak-
> ing and to bear it, if necessary, to the end of our lives
> together.
>
> I have loved you dearly as a sweetheart and will
> continue to love you as my wife. But over and above
> that, I love you with a Christian love that demands that
> I never react in any way toward you that would jeop-
> ardize our prospects of entering heaven, which is the

supreme objective of both our lives. And I pray that God Himself will make our affection for one another perfect and eternal.

James and Myrtle Dobson enjoyed a loving, committed, fulfilling marriage that began in 1935 and ended with his death in 1977. They never wavered for a moment through all those years. If you approach your own marriage with this determination, you'll establish a stable, rewarding relationship that will last a lifetime.

SMD

Can We Talk?

MEN HAVE A SIX-WORD LIMIT

by Erma Bombeck

I have publicly stated that men speak approximately six words a day in their homes. A few readers have challenged me and want to know what the six words are.

I should have qualified my statement. The six words are not necessarily spoken in sequence, nor are they necessarily spoken to wives.

A friend of mine, for example, has a husband who saves his six words until the Carson show has signed off and she is fast asleep. Then he snaps on all the lights in the bedroom, punches his pillow, shakes her out of a sound slumber and says, "Did you turn off the hose?"(6)

Some men will blow their quota at one time.

They'll garage the car, make tracks to the kitchen, take the lid off the fry pan and announce loudly, "I had it for lunch."(5) Then, realizing he has used only five words, he will add, "Yuck!"

Others will spend a half dozen words in obscenities directed toward Bobby's bicycle in the driveway.

My week gets off to a slow start but builds to a feverish climax.

Monday, Me: "Say something."

Him: "What ya want me to say?"(6)

Tuesday, Me: "What kind of day did you have?"

Him: "Don't aggravate me. You wouldn't believe."(6)

Wednesday, Me: "Try me."

Him: "Where's the rest of the paper?"(6)

Thursday, Me: "We had a crisis here today."

Him: "The dog isn't lost, is he?"(6)

Friday, Me: "Guess what? Know who called today? And is coming to dinner? And is bringing her new husband with her? And can't wait to talk your arm off? Are you ready?"

Him: "No. No. No. No. No. No."(6)

Saturday, Me: "I'll be out for a while. I've got some errands to do at the shopping center."

Him: "Admit it. My chattering gets on your nerves."(8)

Sunday, Me: "Do you know you spoke eight words to me yesterday? I wouldn't be surprised if you were starting a new trend."

Him: "Don't count on it."(4)

Part of man's silence is woman's doing. We created the strong, silent, masculine image. The silence represented deep thought, a repression of emotions. A quiet man was an island of mystery, a challenge to probe and discover as years went on. I always thought a quiet man was subtle and romantic.

But that was before I started arguing with the tropical fish over which channel we were going to watch.

LOOKING AHEAD...

The art of communication doesn't come naturally to all of us. Some folks just don't like to talk much. Others talk incessantly without ever really saying anything. But when it comes to marriage, communication is one of *the* keys to success. Those who master this skill are likely to enjoy a meaningful, fulfilling, productive relationship. Those who continually fail to understand each other, however, often feel isolated and alone. It is a major contributor to divorce.

We'll offer some tips this week that can improve your communication skills. I hope that by next Sunday your daily word count will be at least in the double digits—and even more, that your partner will understand what you say.

JCD

WORDS, WORDS

"We have spoken freely to you, Corinthians,
and opened wide our hearts to you."
2 Corinthians 6:11

*E*very knowledgeable marriage counselor knows that the inability or unwillingness of husbands to reveal their feelings to their wives is one of the most common complaints of women. Research shows that little girls are blessed with greater linguistic ability than little boys; it remains a lifelong talent. As an adult, she is typically far better at expressing her thoughts and feelings. God may have given her 50,000 words per day and her husband only 25,000. He comes home with 24,994 used up and disappears into Monday Night Football; she is dying to expend her remaining 25,000 words and find out what he's thinking, what happened at the office, and, especially, how he feels about her. This difference between him and her—a function of their inherited temperaments—is one of countless ways they are unique.

When communication is a problem, compromise is in order. The clammed-up husband must press himself to open his heart and share his deeper feelings. The frustrated wife must recognize that her man may not be capable of the emotional intimacy she seeks. They must seek to fix what can be improved—and to accept the rest.

Just between us...

- Is it true in our case that the wife has twice as many words to use up each day as the husband?
- Have our communicative differences created problems between us?
- In terms of sharing feelings, how would you like our marriage to change?
- What hinders good communication between us? How can we change?

Lord, help us to celebrate our differences as man and woman while tenderly and joyfully helping each other make the most of our union with every word. Amen.

What Did You Say?

Let the wise listen and add to their learning.
Proverbs 1:5

*M*en may use less speech than women, but both sexes have been accused of not using their sense of hearing. "You never told me that" is a common household refrain.

I (JCD) am reminded of the night my father was preaching at an open tent service. During his sermon, an alley cat decided to take a nap on the platform. My father, who was 6'4", took a step backward and planted his heel squarely on the poor creature's tail. The cat went crazy, scratching and clawing to free himself. But Dad, intent on his message, didn't notice. He later said he thought the screech came from the brakes of automobiles at a nearby stop sign. When my father finally moved his foot, the cat took off like a Saturn rocket.

This story illustrates the communication problem many couples face. For example, a wife "screams" for attention and intimacy but feels that he doesn't even notice. It's not that he can't hear her; it's that he's thinking about something else or is completely misinterpreting her signals. This situation can easily be improved by simply "tuning in" to the station on which your mate is broadcasting. The truth is that careful listening feels so much like love that most of us can hardly tell the difference.

Just between us...

- When we tell each other something that doesn't get through, who is to blame—the "sender," the "receiver," or both?
- What have you wanted to say, but didn't because you couldn't get my attention?
- How could learning to listen better to each other help us listen better to God?

Dear God, teach us the wisdom and grace of listening. Help us to pay attention to each word as though we were listening to You. Amen.

QUICK LISTENING

Everyone should be quick to listen,
slow to speak and slow to become angry.
James 1:19

*T*he ability to listen well is harder than it seems. You may recall this old party game: A girl whispers to the boy next to her a sentence such as "Three cows crossed the road to drink from the stream." The boy then whispers the sentence to another boy sitting next to him, and on the message goes in a circle. By the time the sentence gets back to the person who started it, it's transformed into "Trees grow crusty toadstools to think about steam."

Communication between husband and wife can become equally muddled unless we follow the scriptural wisdom offered in James 1:19: Be quick to listen, slow to speak, and slow to become angry. Author-counselors Chuck and Barb Snyder recommend a "quick listening" technique based on this verse. Following a disagreement, a husband and wife sit down together and fully explain their feelings about the issue. The catch is that the other spouse can't interrupt. Partners may try this and still disagree, but by giving their opinion and listening to their mate's, they'll increase their chances of understanding each other…and of staying best friends.

Just between us…

- Do you sometimes feel that you tell me one thing and I hear something else?
- Do either of us tend to interrupt before the other can fully express himself or herself?
- If we tried "quick listening" after all our disagreements, how might it change our marriage?

Father, we want to put Your truths about listening, speaking, and controlling anger to work in our marriage. We ask You to give us Your grace and strength. Help us to stick with it—and help us to notice the good results! Amen.

WORD PICTURES

Jesus spoke to them again in parables, saying: "The kingdom of heaven is like a king who prepared a wedding banquet for his son."
Matthew 22:1–2

*A*nother extremely useful communication technique is the word picture, described by Gary Smalley and John Trent in their book *The Language of Love*. In one of their examples, a high school teacher and football coach named Jim came home each evening too tired to even talk to his wife, Susan, leaving her frustrated and angry. Finally, Susan told Jim a story about a man who went to breakfast with his fellow coaches. The man ate his favorite omelet, then gathered up some crumbs and put them in a bag. Then he went to lunch with more friends and ate a turkey tenderloin pie and a huge salad. Again, he put a few crumbs in a doggie bag to take with him. When he came home that night, he handed his wife and their two boys the little bags of leftovers.

"That's the way I feel when you come home with nothing left to give," Susan said. "All we get are leftovers. I'm waiting to enjoy a meal with you, hoping for time to talk and laugh and get to know you, longing to communicate with you the way you do every day with the guys. But all we get are doggie bags. Honey, don't you see? We don't need leftovers. We need you."

Susan's word picture brought tears to Jim's eyes and led to positive changes in their marriage. You, too, may find that a graphic word picture is more effective at getting your mate's attention than a torrent of hostile words.

Just between us...

- Why are word pictures often effective?
- Jesus often used word pictures to make a point (e.g., "I am the Good Shepherd"). What word picture describes your feelings about us?

Lord, teach us to share our inner selves with our spouse. Remind us of the great value of this intimate exchange between married lovers. Amen.

TOO MUCH HONESTY

Let your conversation be always full of grace.
Colossians 4:6

*M*ost marriage counselors emphasize communication as a foundation for a healthy relationship: Nothing should be withheld from the marital partner. There is wisdom in that advice, provided it's applied with common sense. It may be honest for a man to tell his wife that he hates her fat legs, her varicose veins, or the way she cooks. It's honest for a woman to dump her anger on her husband and constantly berate him for his shortcomings and failures. But honesty that does not have the best interest of the other person at heart is really a cruel form of selfishness.

Some couples, in their determination to share every thought and opinion, systematically destroy the sweet spark of romance that once drew them together. They've lost any sense of mystique in the relationship.

So how does one express intimate feelings while avoiding too much honesty? Paul's advice to all Christians works especially well for married partners: "Let your conversation be always full of grace."

Just between us...

- Am I sometimes *so* honest with you that my words are hurtful?
- Do you think there should be exceptions to telling "the truth, the whole truth, and nothing but the truth" in marriage?
- We know that God honors truthfulness, so how do we apply this to marital communication?
- In what areas could we use more honesty and in what areas, more grace?

Heavenly Father, we know that truthfulness is Your will for our lives—but please give us the wisdom to know when to speak the truth and when to keep it to ourselves. Amen.

THE CONVERSATION GAME

As a fair exchange...open wide your hearts.
2 Corinthians 6:13

*M*y husband has used a single illustration to help parents teach the art of communication to their children. It might be useful to our female readers, as well, in explaining to their husbands how to talk to them. It goes like this:

Give three tennis balls to your husband and ask him to throw them back one at a time. Instead of returning the balls, however, simply hold them. He'll be left wondering what to do next. Obviously, it isn't much of a game. Then explain your point—good conversation is much like a game of catch. You "throw" an idea or comment to your husband (How was work?), and he tosses it back (Great! I finally finished that project for the boss). If your husband doesn't return it (Work was fine), the game ends. Both players feel awkward and wish they were somewhere else.

Of course, husbands and wives should do more than toss superficial details to each other. They should practice sharing dreams, feelings, marriage, spiritual goals, etc. But it all starts with playing the conversation game.

SMD

A Husband's Role

HEAD OF THE HOUSE

by Thom Hunter

*M*y preteen son Patrick doesn't take many things seriously, but occasionally something grabs hold of him and he just won't let it go. He will question an idea or concept until he is satisfied that society isn't misleading him and that all is right in his world.

I'm never prepared for his persistence.

"Dad, can we go to the movies today?" he asked as we crawled down the optimistically named Northwest Expressway.

"Maybe," I said. "I'll check with Mom when we get home."

"She'll say no," he said. "She'll say we need to clean our rooms, or read a book, or play outside. Or...or something else."

The tires on the van made a couple more rotations.

"Dad?" asked Patrick. "Can we get another hamster?"

What a radical idea. We hadn't a hamster die on us in weeks.

"Well, maybe," I answered. "We'll see what Mom thinks."

I turned off the radio.

"Dad?" came the voice again. "Can we eat out tonight?"

"Probably," I said. "If Mom doesn't already have something planned."

I pushed a cassette tape into the player.

"Dad?" Patrick asked. "Is Mom the head of our house?"

Wham! I felt like I was in a ten-car pileup. My face was turning red. My temperature was rising. I was suddenly feeling closed in by the cars surrounding me. I looked in the rearview mirror. Patrick was perched in the middle of the seat behind me, an innocent little grin on his face.

"Patrick," I said, "I am the head of the household. I make the decisions. And don't you forget it. Understand?"

"Okay," he said. "Does that mean we can eat out, go to the movies, and pick up a new hamster on the way home?"

He'd set me up. And I almost fell for it. He was watering down the parent partnership, looking for a crack in which to stick a wedge, testing a biblical concept, and looking for the advantage in the process.

What do pizza, hamsters, and big-screen fantasy have to do with whether or not I am fulfilling my role as head of the family? I asked myself that question as I zeroed in on the bumper in front of me. I slammed on the brakes and avoided the accident. Fortunately, we were at the expressway's top speed of seven miles an hour.

For scoring purposes, we did eat out and go to the movies that night, but we decided to sell the hamster cage. "We" made those decisions, his mother and I.

This "head of the household" thing is very touchy to me. When I was growing up, there was never any doubt. Mother was the head of the household. But she had never intended it to be that way. She was supposed to have had a partner. She understood the concept of a helpmeet. If my father had been a different kind of man and hadn't left us when I was six years old, she would have made a wonderful complement to him.

"You must be a man," she would tell me when I was a teenager. "Take the responsibility; don't run from the decisions; love your wife; cherish your children."

And be the head of the household.

So I always wanted to be the head of the household: ruler over all I surveyed, supreme commander, father and master of my many loyal subjects. I carried this dream to the altar and later into the delivery room— five times. My kingdom went from squalling to crawling to sprawling all around me.

So, if I am the head of the household, why is the head aching and the house barely holding together? And if I am the head of the household, why do I sometimes go to bed with dishpan hands and worry that I've forgotten to unplug the iron?

If I am the head of the household, why do I have to barter for time to watch a football game on television, promising to ride bikes for two hours in exchange for ten minutes of solitude?

And, if I am the head of the household, why do I have to cut my subjects' plates of meat after I set the table? And why do I have to clear the table and pick up mushy mashed potatoes from the floor with my bare hands while everyone else has dessert they weren't supposed to get unless they ate all their mashed potatoes?

And, if I am the head of the household, why do I have to cover five other bodies before I pull my own blanket up to my own chin; explain away everybody else's nightmares before I take on my own; fluff their pillows and tuck their feet back under the sheets; get them one more drink; and plug in their night-lights?

And if I am the head of the household, why do I have to rub my wife's back before she can go to sleep?

Why, I ask? Why do I have to do all these things? Because I am the head of the household, that's why. If I don't listen…if I am inconsiderate of others…if I make decisions without the input of the wife God gave me…if I try to do it on my own without God, then I may as well forget about being the head of the household.

That's what I'll tell Patrick next trip down the Northwest Expressway. We'll have plenty of time.

LOOKING AHEAD…

Husband, this week is designed especially for you. (But we still want your wife to participate!) Like the author of the story above, do you sometimes struggle with your role as "head of the house"? What exactly does that mean, anyway? It is a controversial topic in today's world, but there are biblical truths on which to base an understanding.

We'll offer some of these principles this week. For tonight, why don't you tell your wife how you define "head of the house"—then ask if she agrees.

JCD

A HOLY PARTNERSHIP

Each one of you also must love his wife as he loves himself.
Ephesians 5:33

To properly define the God-ordained role of husbands, there's no better place to turn than Scripture. The apostle Paul instructs: "Husbands, love your wives, just as Christ loved the church and gave himself up for her to make her holy.… In this same way, husbands ought to love their wives as their own bodies" (Ephesians 5:25–28). Paul also tells us "the husband is the head of the wife as Christ is the head of the church" (Ephesians 5:23).

Here's the bottom line of your responsibility as a husband: You are charged with the holy, loving leadership of your wife. There is *nothing* dictatorial or selfish in this prescription! Your love is to be so strong that it mirrors Christ's love for the church, so committed that you would unquestioningly die to save her, and so powerful that it is indistinguishable from love of your self.

What a challenge! And what a privilege to join with God and your wife in this holy partnership! For as you fulfill your role as head of the house, you'll encounter blessings you never imagined.

Just between us...

- (husband) What has been my most "shining moment" as your husband?
- (husband) Do you feel my love for you meets this scriptural ideal?
- (wife) How do you feel about the responsibility God gives husbands?
- (wife) How can I encourage you in this role?

(husband) *Heavenly Father, You have given me an awesome and holy responsibility to love my wife just as Christ loved the church. Help me to follow His perfect example as I learn to increase my love for my mate. Amen.*

DECISIONS, DECISIONS

*The head of every man is Christ, and the head of
the woman is man, and the head of Christ is God.*

1 Corinthians 11:3

*A*mong the most controversial Scriptures are those relating to a wife's obligation to "submit" to a husband's leadership. This principle offends many women. Futhermore, it places power in the hands of men who sometimes misuse it. And yet, there it is, time and again: "The husband is head of the wife." Those words can't be brushed aside by those who rely on Scripture as their infallible guide. But what does this "headship" really mean?

The Bible makes it clear that the husband is to be the leader in his home, yet he has no right to run roughshod over the opinions and feelings of his wife. He is to love her as Christ loved the church (Ephesians 5:25) and to serve her unselfishly and compassionately. A man should include his wife in making mutually satisfying decisions, always working to incorporate her perspectives and seeking compromise when possible. In situations where they simply cannot find common ground, Scripture gives the man the prerogative—and responsibility—to choose and lead. Yet in this case, he must be more sensitive and considerate than ever, bearing in mind that he will ultimately answer to God not only for his choices, but for his treatment of his wife.

Just between us...

- (husband) How would you rate my leadership as your husband?
- Does our decision-making process fit the biblical model?
- (wife) How do you feel about your role as "leader in the home"?
- (husband) Am I sensitive to your feelings regarding decisions?

Heavenly Father, in Your divine plan for marriage You have asked the husband to lead and the wife to submit, and we want so much to obey You. We come humbly now, asking for Your wisdom and help to do so. Amen.

The Single Man

*Pity the man who falls and
has no one to help him up!*
Ecclesiastes 4:10

Contrary to conventional wisdom, the single man often has a rough go of life. He is far more likely than an unmarried female to be an alcoholic, drug user, or convicted criminal. He is less responsible about his driving habits, finances, and personal appearance. (Check with your auto insurance agent, bank officer, or neighbor with college-age sons if you doubt this statement.)

There are millions of exceptions, of course, but statistically speaking, an unmarried young man is at risk for many antisocial behaviors. Yet when he falls in love, marries, and begins to care for, protect, and support his wife, he becomes a mainstay of social order. His selfish impulses are inhibited. His sexual passions are channeled. He discovers a sense of pride in his family. He learns why, on average, a married man lives a longer and happier life than his single counterpart.

God knew what He was doing when He designed the institution of marriage. It's a smart husband who recognizes this and lovingly cultivates his relationship with his wife.

Just between us...

- Do you feel you changed after we married?
- Do you ever miss being single? Why?
- How has being married to me benefited your life?
- How can I help you feel more joy in our marriage and pride in our family?

(husband) *Dear God, thank You for Your gift to me of marriage. Thank You for my lovely spouse and for Your daily blessing on our relationship and our home. May I never take Your generosity for granted or Your holy purposes lightly. Amen.*

THE RENEGADE MALE

Fathers, do not exasperate your children; instead, bring
them up in the training and instruction of the Lord.
Ephesians 6:4

uthor Derek Prince has described the "renegade male" as one of society's biggest problems. The word *renegade* actually means "one who has shirked his primary responsibilities." It is an accurate description of those husbands and fathers who pour every resource into work or pleasure, leaving the child-rearing task entirely to their wives. Both boys and girls desperately need their fathers, who have a specific role to play in their lives.

Research in the field of child development has confirmed that the absence of positive masculine influence plays a key role in adolescent rebellion, sex-role identity, and cohesion within the family. Conversely, those who accept their God-given responsibilities at home have a fleeting—and golden—opportunity to shape the little lives entrusted to their care.

Just between us...

- (husband) Do I ever resemble a renegade male? How?
- (husband) In what ways have I been a good father? (For couples without children: What kind of father would I be?)
- (wife) How have our own fathers been good or poor examples of fulfilling their responsibilities at home?
- (wife) How, as a wife, can I help you be a better father?

(husband) *Dear God, thank You for the responsibility and opportunity to impact my children for good. I want to be faithful. Help me to celebrate—not resent—my fatherly duties. Through my sometimes inadequate efforts, accomplish great things in the lives of my kids. Amen.*

A WIFE'S COUNTENANCE

He is to be free to stay at home and bring
happiness to the wife he has married.
Deuteronomy 24:5

*I*f you really want to know about a man and what kind of character he has, you need only look at the countenance of his wife. Everything he has invested, or withheld, will be there."

That was the message Bill McCartney, then head coach of the University of Colorado football team, heard in a 1994 sermon. The words cut straight to his heart. McCartney had built the Colorado football program into a powerhouse that won a national championship in 1990. He had also cofounded a national men's movement, Promise Keepers. But those achievements came at a price. For years McCartney had withheld his time and energy from his wife, Lyndi, and their four children. In 1994 Bill McCartney didn't like what he saw in Lyndi's countenance—so he resigned his position at Colorado to devote more time to his wife and family.

As a husband, you bear the primary responsibility for your wife's welfare and emotional well-being. What do you see in her face tonight?

Just between us...

- (husband) Do you ever feel like you're competing for my attention?
- (husband) Do I appear preoccupied by my work or recreational activities?
- (wife) What do you imagine it was like for Bill McCartney to walk away from his successful coaching career?
- (wife) Do you ever struggle with trying to care for my emotional well-being? Is there anything I can do to help?

(husband) *Almighty God, with Your help I wholeheartedly accept my responsibility to care for my wife's emotional well-being. May I increasingly become a master at it, so that I can see joy and contentment in her face. Amen.*

A SPIRITUAL LEADER

*For I have chosen him, so that he will direct his children
and his household after him to keep the way of the LORD.*
Genesis 18:19

*P*erhaps the most important aspect of a husband's headship in
the home is his role as spiritual leader. When all is said and
done, can there be anything more important to a husband
than promoting the spiritual health of his wife and children while on
earth and being reunited with them in heaven?

One of the things that has impressed me most about Jim during all
these years is his dedication to our family's spiritual life and the example
he has set for me, Danae, and Ryan. Our first date was a Sunday evening
church service, and he has never wavered from his commitment to
church, especially in terms of tithing and attendance. So many times
when our children were still at home, Jim would return from a trip late
Saturday night or early Sunday morning, then get up and go to Sunday
school. I know he was dead on his feet from fatigue, but he didn't want
his kids to see him lying in bed on the Sabbath. Early in our marriage,
Jim also established routines for family devotionals, prayer time, and
Bible study (admittedly at times more consistently than others). That was
such a blessing for our children as they grew up in the Lord and was, and
is, so encouraging to me.

Husbands, I urge you to take stock of your family's spiritual life. Are
you setting the proper example? Are you establishing times for you, your
wife, and your kids to mature in God's Word? You may stumble occasionally as you nuture your family's faith, just as we have, but I encourage you to be a husband who stays the course. That's the kind of leader
your wife wants and needs—and the kind the Lord desires as well.

SMD

A Wife's Role

MARTHA'S SECRET INGREDIENT

by Roy J. Reiman

t bothered Ben every time he walked through the kitchen. It was that little metal container on the shelf above Martha's cookstove. He probably would not have noticed it so much or been bothered by it if Martha had not repeatedly told him never to touch it. The reason, she said, was that it contained a "secret herb" from her mother, and since she had no way of refilling the container, she was concerned that if Ben or anyone else ever picked it up and looked inside, they might accidentally drop it and spill its valuable contents.

The container wasn't really much to look at. It was so old that much of its original red and gold floral pattern had faded. You could tell right where it had been gripped again and again when the container was lifted and its tight lid pulled off. Not only Martha's fingers had gripped it there; her mother's and her grandmother's had, too. Martha didn't know for sure, but she thought that perhaps even her great-grandmother had used this same container and its "secret herb."

All Ben knew for certain was that shortly after he had married Martha, her mother had brought the container to Martha and told her to make the same loving use of its contents as she had.

And she did, faithfully. Ben never saw Martha cook a dish without taking the container off the shelf and sprinkling just a little of the secret herb over the ingredients. Even when she baked cakes, pies, and cookies, she added a light sprinkling just before she put the pans in the oven.

Whatever was in that container, it sure worked, for Ben thought that Martha was the best cook in the world. He wasn't alone in that opinion—anyone who ever ate at their house grandly praised Martha's cooking.

But why wouldn't she let Ben touch that little container? Was she really afraid he'd spill its contents? And what did that secret herb look like? It was so fine that whenever Martha sprinkled it over the food she was preparing, Ben couldn't quite make out its texture. She obviously had to use very little of it because there was no way to refill the container.

Somehow Martha had stretched those contents over thirty years of marriage, and it had never failed to effect mouth-watering results.

Ben became increasingly tempted to look into that container just once, but he never brought himself to do so.

Then one day Martha became ill. Ben took her to the hospital, where they kept her overnight. When he returned home, he found it extremely lonely in the house. Martha had never been gone overnight before. And when it neared suppertime, he wondered what to do—Martha had so loved to cook that he had never bothered to learn much about preparing food.

When he wandered into the kitchen to see what was in the refrigerator, he immediately saw the container on the shelf. His eyes were drawn to it like a magnet. He quickly looked away, but his curiosity drew him back.

What was in that container? Why wasn't he to touch it? What did that secret herb look like? How much of it was left?

Ben looked away again and lifted the cover of a large cake pan on the kitchen counter. Ahh...there was more than half of one of Martha's great cakes left. He cut off a large piece, sat down at the kitchen table, and hadn't taken more than one bite when his eyes went back to that container again. What would it hurt if he looked inside? Why was Martha so secretive about that container, anyway?

Ben took another bite and debated with himself—should he or shouldn't he? For five more big bites he thought about it, staring at the container. Finally he could no longer resist.

He walked slowly across the room and ever so carefully took the container off the shelf, fearing that—horror of horrors—he'd spill the contents while sneaking a peek.

He set the container on the counter and carefully pried off the lid. He was almost scared to look inside! When the inside of the container came into full view, Ben's eyes opened wide. Why, the container was empty—except for a little folded scrap of paper at the bottom.

Ben reached down for the paper, struggling to get his big rugged hand inside. He carefully picked it up by a corner, removed it, and slowly unfolded it under the kitchen light.

A brief note was scrawled inside, and Ben immediately recognized the handwriting as that of Martha's mother. Very simply it said: "Martha—To everything you make, add a dash of love."

Ben swallowed hard, replaced the note and the container, and quietly went back to finishing his cake. Now he completely understood why it tasted so good.

LOOKING AHEAD...

Even though for the first thirty years of their marriage, Ben couldn't quite identify his wife's "secret herb," he knew it was there—and that it made a wonderful difference in his wife's cooking. If you're the wife in the marriage partnership, I suspect that you have added your own secret ingredient to many aspects of your marriage.

We'll be talking about the role of a wife this week and offering several definitions, but most of it boils down to this: As you help and care for your husband, add a dash of love to everything you do.

JCD

A Suitable Helper

The LORD God made a woman from the rib he had
taken out of the man, and he brought her to the man.
Genesis 2:22

rom the beginning, God was clear about a woman's primary role in this world. Genesis 2:18 reads: "It is not good for the man to be alone. I will make a helper suitable for him." No one took her role as helper more seriously than Jane Hill, late wife of Los Angeles pastor E. V. Hill. She loved him deeply and devoted herself to his needs. E. V. once received a death threat from gang members indicating he would be killed the next day. He woke up the following morning "thankful to be alive," as he told it later. "But I noticed that [Jane] was gone. I looked out my window, and my car was gone. I went outside and finally saw her driving up, still in her robe. I said, 'Where have you been?' She said, 'I...I...it just occurred to me that they [could have] put a bomb in that car last night, and if you had gotten in there you would have been blown away. So I got up and drove it. It's all right.'"

A man is fortunate indeed when his wife is his devoted helper—whether she bakes him a cake, soothes his aching muscles, or even puts her life on the line for him. No role demonstrates more beautifully the way Jesus shows His love for each of us.

Just between us...

- (husband) Does the role of "helper" seem insulting to you?
- (husband) Is it easy for you to "serve" me as your husband?
- (husband) Do I notice and respond when you do?
- (wife) Which aspect of my support means the most to you?

(wife) Dear Lord, thank You for creating me to help and serve my husband. I embrace this ministry with all my heart! Grant me Your wisdom, strength, and joy in this calling. Bless him through my every word and deed. Amen.

BELIEVE IN HIM

The wife must respect her husband.
Ephesians 5:33

*T*he male ego is surprisingly fragile, especially during times of failure and embarrassment. It's one of the reasons why a husband desperately needs his wife's support and respect.

Jane Hill clearly understood this aspect of a wife's role. Over Jane's objections, E. V. once invested his family's scarce resources in the purchase of a service station. Jane opposed the decision because she knew that her husband lacked the time and expertise to oversee his investment. She was right; the station went broke. When E. V. called to say he'd lost the station, Jane could have said, "I told you so" and crushed his spirit. He could have been humiliated in that moment of vulnerability. Instead, she said, "If you smoked and drank, you would have lost as much as you lost in the service station. So it's six in one hand and a half-dozen in the other. Let's forget it."

A wife can "make" or "break" a man. If she believes in her husband and has confidence in his leadership, he typically gains the confidence he needs to take risks and use his assets wisely. But if she is competitive, critical, and disrespectful of her husband, she becomes a liability to the entire family. Read Ephesians 5:33 again. One of the most important keys to a successful marriage is found in a single word: *respect!*

Just between us...

- (wife) Do you feel that I believe in you?
- (wife) What do you think is the biggest setback or failure you've experienced? Did I show support at that time?
- (wife) How can I better show respect to you?

(wife) Heavenly Father, forgive me for the times I have not shown my husband respect. I want to increase his self-confidence, not diminish it. Please show me how to become that kind of godly wife. Amen.

THE SUBMISSION DEBATE

Wives, submit to your husbands as to the Lord.
Ephesians 5:22

*T*here's no quicker way to disrupt a festive gathering of Christian women than to bring up the topic of *submission*. Before you know it, friends start facing off to launch passionate discourses on all sides of the issue. Either that or they laugh contemptuously. Yet God's direction on the subject is clear: "The head of every man is Christ, and the head of every woman is man, and the head of Christ is God" (1 Corinthians 11:3).

Each of us submits to a higher authority. Consider the boss at work or the IRS agent at tax time. They are our equals as people, yet we submit to them because they have authority over us when they assume certain roles. A wife submits to her husband in the same manner. You both are equally valued, equally important partners—yet your roles are different. Furthermore, submission cannot be understood or appreciated apart from the other half of the prescription found in Ephesians 5:25, which requires a husband to love his wife as Christ loved the church, to the point of *giving up his life for her.* There is no room for inconsiderateness, oppression, or domination here!

As a wife, you are asked to submit to the leadership of your husband. As a husband, you are told to sacrificially love and cherish your wife. It is the divine plan for marriage and family.

Just between us...

- How do we define a wife's duty to submit to her husband?
- (wife) How well do you think I follow God's direction in this area?
- How can we help each other with submission as defined by God?

(wife) Father, I admit, submission doesn't always come easily to me. But I accept Your wonderful plan for our marriage. Today I look for Your abundant blessing as I wholeheartedly support my husband as the head of our marriage. Amen.

NOBLE CHARACTER

A wife of noble character is her husband's crown,
but a disgraceful wife is like decay in his bones.
Proverbs 12:4

A girl named Lucy gained something of a reputation for her deceitful nature. Countless times she persuaded a boy named Charlie Brown to try to kick the football she was holding, and each time she snatched it away just before he could boot it.

In the comic strips or in real life, a deceitful woman is best avoided. Solomon described such a wife as "decay in his bones." The king must have known many a troublesome woman, for he also declared, "Better to live on a corner of the roof than share a house with a quarrelsome wife" (Proverbs 21:9). The Bible lists many other examples of women who showed disgraceful behavior, including Eve and Lot's wife (disobedient), Michal (critical), Jezebel (unscrupulous and violent), Job's wife (foolish), Herodias (cruel), and Sapphira (greedy).

Temptation will come to even the most spiritual among us, but the wife who holds fast to her noble character will bring glory to God and blessings to her husband and herself.

Just between us...

- (wife) If you were asked to describe my character, would the word *noble* come to mind? Why or why not?
- What is noble character, and how can it bring glory to God? (You might consider some examples of noble women in the Bible—Ruth, Abigail, Mary of Bethany, and Mary, the mother of Jesus.)
- How can you and I teach noble character to the next generation?

(wife) Dear Father, help me to receive the teaching of Your Word: It's noble character—not youth, beauty, charm, or wealth—that will make me a priceless crown to my husband. Help me to be that kind of wife in word and deed. Amen.

CAMPING COMPANIONS

Just as you share in our sufferings,
so also you share in our comfort.
2 Corinthians 1:7

After learning that camping was a common pastime among happy families, Gary Smalley and his wife, Norma, decided to take their own brood into the wild. On a beautiful Kentucky night, the Smalleys gathered around a campfire, sang songs, and roasted hot dogs. By nine o'clock all were pleasantly tired and tucked into their camper beds. Gary thought, *I can really see why this draws families together.*

Then it struck. Thunder rolled and lightning flashed all around. Rain and wind assaulted the outside, then the inside, of the Smalley camper. The sudden storm turned what had been a relaxing evening into a night of fright.

Did this harrowing turn of events cause Gary and Norma to abandon the outdoors forever? Not at all—they became avid campers. The Smalleys discovered that sharing experiences, both fun *and* frightful, bonded them in ways they couldn't have imagined.

Our encouragement to couples is to share each others' interests and activities. Common endeavors will deepen your relationship and provide priceless family memories—even when storms strike.

Just between us...

- How does sharing recreation and other interests build companionship?
- (husband) Which of my favorite activities do you enjoy?
- (wife) Do you appreciate having me join you in your activities? Which ones, and why?
- What new shared activities could bring us closer together?

Lord, thank You for tonight's encouragement to be friends and companions in many ways. Show us new ways to get the most out of life—together! Amen.

THAT PROVERBS 31 WOMAN...

A woman who fears the LORD is to be praised.
Proverbs 31:30

*A*re you ever intimidated by the "Proverbs 31 woman"? Sometimes I am. How can we compete? Here's a woman who brings her husband "good, not harm, all the days of her life"; gets up before the morning light; feeds her family; shows good judgment in her purchases; works "vigorously"; helps the poor; has time to make bed coverings for her household and garments for sale; has enough faith to "laugh at the days to come"; "speaks with wisdom"; has no use for idleness; and earns blessing and praise from her husband and children!

Let's be honest, we can't compete...but maybe we don't have to. I'm not convinced, for example, that the woman described in Proverbs 31 is one literal person. Or, if she is, that she achieved all her accomplishments during the same period of life. Rather, I think that through the writings of Solomon, the Lord has provided us women with specific examples of the behavior to which we should continually aspire—just as all Christians aspire to be like Jesus, even though we'll never actually reach His level of perfection.

I believe that the key to understanding Proverbs 31 is found in verse 30, the next to last passage in Proverbs: "Charm is deceptive, and beauty is fleeting, but a woman who fears the LORD is to be praised." According to this verse, a "woman who fears the LORD,"—who seeks His will for her as wife, mother, and follower of Jesus—*is* the Proverbs 31 woman, no matter how a particular day or season of her life is going.

My encouragement to you as a wife is to seek God and submit to His direction—and add a dash of love in the process. I promise you that you'll please your Maker, bring honor to your husband and family, and find a personal contentedness that will never be matched.

SMD

His Unfailing Presence

That's the Way I Feel about You

by Nancy Jo Sullivan

O ne hot July morning, I awoke to the clicks of a broken fan blowing humid air across my face. The well-used fan had seen better days. It had only one setting, and its blades were worn and bent. It needed repair. So, I thought, did my life.

Earlier that year Sarah, our Down's syndrome daughter, had undergone heart surgery. That was behind us, but now we faced mounting medical bills that insurance wouldn't cover. On top of that, my husband's job would be eliminated in just weeks, and losing our home seemed inevitable.

As I closed my eyes to try to put together a morning prayer, I felt a small hand nudge my arm. "Mommy," Sarah said, "I g-g-got r-r-ready for v-v-vacation B-B-Bible school all by myself!"

Next to the bed stood five-year-old Sarah, her eyes twinkling through thick, pink-framed glasses. Beaming, she turned both palms up and exclaimed, "Ta-dah!"

Her red-checked, seersucker shorts were on backward, with the drawstring stuck in the side waistband. A J. C. Penney price tag hung from a new, green polka-dot top. It was inside out. She had chosen one red and one green winter sock to go with the outfit. Her tennis shoes were on the wrong feet, and she wore a baseball cap with the visor and emblem turned backward.

"I-I-I packed a b-b-backpack, t-t-too!" she stuttered while unzipping her bag so I could see what was inside. Curious, I peered in at the treasures she had so carefully packed: five Lego blocks, an unopened box of paper clips, a fork, a naked Cabbage Patch doll, three jigsaw puzzle pieces, and a crib sheet from the linen closet.

Gently lifting her chin until our eyes met, I said very slowly, "You look beautiful!"

"Thank y-y-you." Sarah smiled as she began to twirl around like a ballerina.

Just then the living room clock chimed eight, which meant I had forty-five minutes to get Sarah, a toddler, and a baby out the door. As I hurried to feed the kids while rocking a crying infant, the morning minutes dissolved into urgent seconds. I knew I was not going to have time to change Sarah's outfit.

Buckling each child into a car seat, I tried to reason with Sarah. "Honey, I don't think you'll be needing your backpack for vacation Bible school. Why don't you let me keep it in the car for you."

"No-o-o-o. I n-n-need it!"

I finally surrendered, telling myself her self-esteem was more important than what people might think of her knapsack full of useless stuff.

When we got to church, I attempted to redo Sarah's outfit with one hand while I held my baby in the other. But Sarah pulled away, reminding me of my early morning words, "No-o-o-o...I l-l-look beautiful!"

Overhearing our conversation, a young teacher joined us. "You do look beautiful!" the woman told Sarah. Then she took Sarah's hand and said to me, "You can pick up Sarah at 11:30. We'll take good care of her." As I watched them walk away, I knew Sarah was in good hands.

While Sarah was in school, I took the other two children and ran errands. As I dropped late payments into the mailbox and shopped with coupons at the grocery store, my thoughts raced with anxiety and disjointed prayer. What did the future hold? How would we provide for our three small children? Would we lose our home? Does God really care about us?

I got back to the church a few minutes early. A door to the sun-filled chapel had been propped open, and I could see the children seated inside in a semicircle listening to a Bible story.

Sarah, sitting with her back to me, was still clutching the canvas straps that secured her backpack. Her baseball cap, shorts, and shirt were still on backwards and inside out.

As I watched her, one simple thought came to mind: "I sure do love her."

As I stood there, I heard that still, comforting voice that I have come to understand is God's: "That's the way I feel about you."

I closed my eyes and imagined my Creator looking at me from a distance: my life so much like Sarah's outfit—backward, unmatched, mixed up.

"Why are you holding that useless 'backpack' full of anxiety, doubt, and fear?" I could imagine God saying to me. "Let Me carry it."

That night as I once again turned on our crippled fan, I felt a renewed sense of hope. Sarah had reminded me that God's presence remains even when life needs repair. I might not have the answers to all my problems—but I would always be able to count on Him to help carry the load.

LOOKING AHEAD...

Thanks to her five-year-old daughter, Nancy Jo Sullivan rediscovered the reality of God's all-powerful presence. Many never understand that He is in our midst, ready to love us and pick up our backpacks full of troubles and fears. These people doubt, neglect to ask for His help, or fail to see how the Lord provides in their time of need. But He is there—the Unfailing Presence—always watching, always ready to share in our strife and lovingly guide us, no matter how difficult our circumstances.

When hardship and crises strike, you may be tempted to feel that God has let you down or no longer cares. Resist this thinking! Even when His solution is not the one you seek, be assured that it is just what you need for the trials you face.

We'll spend this week talking about the trustworthiness of the Lord. Sooner or later in every Christian marriage, it's a truth that matters more than life itself!

JCD

THE WHEELBARROW OF TRUST

I will trust and not be afraid.
Isaiah 12:2

Most of us struggle to "be anxious for nothing," but we can learn to rely on God if we know the difference between faith and trust.

Let's imagine you're near the beautiful but dangerous Niagara Falls. A circus performer has strung a rope across the falls with the intention of pushing a wheelbarrow from one side to the other. Just before stepping on the rope, he asks you, "Do you think I can accomplish this feat?"

His reputation has preceded him, so you reply that you believe he can walk the tightrope. In other words, you have *faith* that he will succeed. Then he says, "If you really believe I can do it, how about getting in the wheelbarrow and crossing with me?" Accepting his invitation would be an example of remarkable *trust*.

It isn't difficult for some people to believe that God is capable of performing mighty deeds. After all, He created the entire universe. Trust, however, requires that we depend on Him to keep His promises to us even when there is no proof that He will. It's not so easy to get into that wheelbarrow and put our lives in His care. Yet it's a step we must take if we are to "be anxious for nothing" in all of life's circumstances.

Just between us...

- Do you find it easy or difficult to trust God?
- Have you ever felt that the Lord has abandoned you, or that He hasn't heard your prayer? How did you deal with that feeling?
- How could putting our trust in God help our marriage?

Dear Lord, You alone are worthy of our complete trust. But responding to You in trust is often difficult. Teach us to trust You—to lean on Your strength, to count on Your goodness, and to expect Your faithfulness always. Amen.

WORDS YOU CAN COUNT ON

I have put my hope in your laws.
Psalm 119:43

*J*ust as you must trust the Lord in all you do, so also should you trust His Word.

Years ago, shortly after I (JCD) left my positions at Children's Hospital of Los Angeles and the University of Southern California School of Medicine, I discovered that my frequent travel and speaking engagements on behalf of families were taking a toll on my own family. As I wrestled with this problem, I came across a Scripture passage that showed me the solution. Moses was exhausted from solving all his people's disputes. Jethro, his father-in-law, recognized this and advised Moses to appoint others to help, saying "If you do this, and God so commands, you will be able to stand the strain, and all these people will go home satisfied" (Exodus 18:23). The next day I canceled all but two of my speaking appointments for the following year and determined to stay home. That decision led to the start of Focus on the Family and a film series seen by 80 million people!

The wisdom contained in the world's leading bestseller—the Bible—has sustained husbands and wives for thousands of years. Wouldn't it be foolish to trust God, yet ignore His Word?

Just between us...

- What Scripture verse has made the biggest difference in your life?
- Do you feel that we spend enough time reading the Bible as a couple?
- How can we allocate more time for reading the Word?
- Which book of the Bible would you like to study next?
- How can we get even more out of our Scripture reading?

Dear God, thank You so much for giving us a trustworthy, written guide to show us how we should live. Help us to increasingly rely on the Bible for Your wisdom for our lives. Amen.

SET UP FOR DISAPPOINTMENT

Do not put your trust in princes,
in mortal men, who cannot save.
Psalm 146:3

*T*he media continually bombard us with images of broken trust: spouses who cheat on each other; politicians who break promises; corporate chiefs who steal from their employees. The list goes on and on.

People in positions of responsibility *should* be held accountable to the highest moral and ethical standards. Yet each of these people is a mortal creature with a natural bent toward sin. The minute we begin placing our deepest faith and trust in human beings, we set ourselves up for severe disappointment.

What does this mean for marriage? Even in the best of relationships, husbands and wives may err and break the other's trust. That's why we must rely on God's power—not our own—to lead honorable lives. When husbands and wives commit themselves to live according to God's ways, a bond of trust develops between them. Though none of us is perfect, we can give our heart confidently to our spouse when we know that he or she is genuinely seeking to follow God and His guidelines.

Just between us...

- Has someone in a position of responsibility ever broken your trust?
- Is it ever difficult for you to trust me?
- Knowing our sinful nature, how can we still earn each other's trust?
- How do you think the Lord blesses spouses who trust each other?
- How might we develop an even deeper level of trust in our relationship?

Heavenly Father, thank You that You are completely worthy of our trust. As my spouse and I commit ourselves to being trustworthy with each other, empower us by Your Spirit. Grant us grace when we fail. And bless us, we pray, with joy and confidence as we make trustworthiness a priority. Amen.

THE MARRIAGE TRIANGLE

"Blessed is the man who trusts in the LORD."
Jeremiah 17:7

od promises to bless those who trust in Him. The Psalms state that joy, deliverance, triumph, mercy, provision, blessedness, safety, and usefulness will come to those who put their confidence in the Lord.

We need to rely on those blessings in our marriages—otherwise the stresses of life will pull us apart. And those stresses *will* come! When the house burns down…when a child becomes ill…when a job and steady paycheck are lost, it's all too easy to let fear and frustration drive a wedge between partners. Even minor problems, such as a nagging cold or a sleepless night, can disrupt the quality of our marriage.

The good news is that we weren't meant to succeed by depending only on each other. Marriage is a triangle—with husband and wife at the bottom corners and the Lord at the top. The book of Ecclesiastes conveys a similar truth when Solomon talks about the strength of a three-stranded cord (4:12). If we invite the Lord into our marriage and trust in His strength, we can experience strength and peace in our marriage regardless of the circumstances.

Just between us...

- When, before our marriage, did God prove strong for you in a time of crisis? What specific blessing did He provide?
- How has He blessed us during hard times in our marriage?
- What are some of the little stresses that tend to drive us apart?
- In light of what we've read this week, how can we encourage each other to trust God more?

Dear Lord, we praise You that You—the God of love, power, and goodness—want to be a powerful presence in our relationship. When testings come, bind us together with love. When we are weak, be strong for us. Amen.

TIMES OF PLENTY

I have set the LORD always before me.
Psalm 16:8

*J*ust as we're tempted to think God has forgotten about us when hard times come, so we tend to forget God when times are easy. Think about the marriages you have seen slide into trouble just when the couples seemed to have everything going their way.

Jesus told a story about a rich farmer who had no need for God. The farmer had his life nicely laid out. One year he produced such a bumper crop that he couldn't store it all. In a world of suffering and starvation, that was his biggest problem! Then he said, "This is what I'll do. I will tear down my barns and build bigger ones, and there I will store all my grain and my goods. And I'll say to myself, 'You have plenty of good things laid up for many years. Take life easy; eat, drink, and be merry.'" But God said to him, "You fool! This very night your life will be demanded from you. Then who will get what you have prepared for yourself?" (Luke 12:18–20).

Are you in a time of relative plenty in your life together? If so, be careful about slipping into arrogance and self-contentedness. The next thing you know you'll be behaving like the fool in Jesus' story—as if you don't need God. An old-time preacher once wrote, "Blessedness is the greatest of perils because it tends to dull our keen sense of dependence on God and make us prone to presumption."

Take a moment tonight to thank and praise God for all the good you enjoy. And remember to fully depend on Him each day, even when everything is going wonderfully.

Just between us...

- Do we trust God in good times, or do we begin to feel self-sufficient?
- Do we give God the credit and praise when life is good?
- How can we encourage each other to rely on the Lord at *all* times?

Lord, You have poured out Your goodness on our lives, and we are truly grateful. Forgive us when we let satisfaction dull our devotion to You. Amen.

No Fear

"Do not let your hearts be troubled. Trust in God."

John 14:1

When Focus on the Family was in its early stages and our children were young, Jim often traveled. One night when he was away, I awoke with a start at 2 A.M. I was afraid and didn't know why. After a few minutes of worrying, I forced myself out of bed and sank to my knees on the floor.

"Oh, Lord," I prayed, "I don't know why I'm so frightened. I ask You to watch over our home and protect our family. Send Your guardian angel to be with us." I climbed back into bed and fell asleep about a half hour later.

The next morning one of our teenage neighbors ran over from across the street. "Mrs. Dobson, did you hear what happened? A burglar robbed your next-door neighbor's house last night!" It was true. A thief had broken in and escaped with the family's vacation money, about $500. Then my neighbor told me that the police had determined the time of the robbery—about 2 A.M., the same time I had awakened in fear!

My mind reeled at the thought. "If a burglar wanted to break into our house," I said, "he would probably try to get in through the bathroom window near our children's bedrooms. Let's go look." We walked to the window and saw that the screen was bent and the window sill splintered. Someone had indeed tried to break in. What had stopped him?

I am convinced that God protected us that night through my panicked prayer. In a frantic moment my trust was tested and God again proved faithful. I can't explain why He sometimes allows us to experience fearful situations even though we are praying. But I know that even in those threatening circumstances, He is "an ever-present help in trouble" (Psalm 46:1). That is why we can say, with the psalmist, "We will not fear.... The Lord Almighty is with us" (Psalm 46:2, 7).

SMD

That Lovin' Feeling

ROMANCE

by Bill and Lynne Hybels

R omance was never my strong suit. I proposed to Lynne in her parents' garage; I took my Harley-Davidson on our honeymoon; I thought our best anniversary was the one we spent watching a video of *Rocky III*. I had to learn the gentle art of romance.

For starters, I figured it meant flowers. Beyond that, I didn't have a clue, but I knew I could get the flower job done. As confirmation from God that I was moving in the right direction, who do you think set up shop right out of the trunk of his '58 DeSoto at the corner opposite our church? The flower man!

So, quite regularly, on my way home from work or meetings, I would pull over to the side of the road, buy a bunch of roses or carnations from the flower man, and take them home to Lynne. *What a husband!* I thought as I handed over my three bucks.

Yet when I proudly presented the flowers to Lynne, fully expecting her to hire the Marine Corps Band to play "Hail to the Chief," her response was lukewarm.

"Gee, thanks," she said. "Where'd you get these?"

"Where else? My buddy, the flower man—you know, the guy with the '58 DeSoto at Barrington and Algonquin. I'm a volume buyer now. I stop there so often that he gives me a buck off, and if they're a little wilted, he gives me two bucks off. I figure they'll perk up when you put them in water."

"Of course," she said.

I kept it up consistently for quite a while—until Lynne's lack of enthusiasm for the gift drained my enthusiasm.

Some time later, on our regularly scheduled date night, Lynne and I decided to clear the air of anything that might be bothering either of us. We do that now and then. We sat down in a cheap restaurant (not only am I unromantic, I'm also Dutch) and asked, "What's going on? Is there anything we need to talk about? Is there anything amiss in our relationship?"

On that particular evening, Lynne took out her list and started checking off the items.

"Ooooh, you're right on that one. Eeeh, that one, too. Yep. Guilty as charged. Guilty. Guilty. You're right again."

She ended her list, and I was in a pile.

"I really am sorry," I said, "but trust me. I'm going to do better."

"Now, what about you?" she asked.

I really didn't have any complaints, but after hearing her list, I thought I should say *something*. I scrambled.

"Well, I do have one little problem. Have you noticed the absence of the flowers lately?"

"No," she said. "I haven't really paid attention."

How could she say that?

"We have a problem," I said. "I can't figure it out. Hundreds of thousands of husbands pass by that corner. Do they stop for flowers? No. Do I stop? Yes! What gives? What is your problem?"

Her answer made my head spin. She looked me straight in the eyes and said quietly, "The truth is, Bill, I'm not impressed when you give me half-dead flowers that come out of the trunk of a '58 DeSoto that you were lucky enough to run across on your way home from work. The flowers are cheap, and the effort is minimal. The way I see it, you're not investing enough time or energy to warrant a wholehearted response from me. You're not thinking about what would make me happy; you're just doing what's convenient for you."

"Okay, let's get this straight," I said. "You would be happier if I got up from my desk in the middle of my busy day, threw my study schedule to the wind, walked all the way across the parking lot, got in my car, and made a special trip to Barrington, where I'd have to pay quadruple the price just because it said Barrington on the bag? And you wouldn't mind if the extra time it took crimped my workout schedule at the Y.... And you wouldn't mind if I came home late because of all the extra running around I would have to do to get you expensive flowers? Is that what you're telling me? That would make you happy?"

Without batting an eyelash, Lynne said, "Yes, that would make me happy."

I couldn't believe it! "What are you talking about? What you're asking for is impractical, uneconomical, and an inefficient use of time."

"That's a great definition of romance, Bill. You're learning!"

LOOKING AHEAD...

Whether we've been with our partner for one year or forty, we're all still trying to master the definition—and execution—of romance in our marriages. As Bill Hybels learned, there's far more to romantic love than meets the eye. What his wife needed was a heart-to-heart and soul-to-soul relationship. This kind of relationship seems natural to women, but sometimes men have a hard time figuring it out.

So just what *is* romance? We'll talk about that in the week ahead. For tonight, spend a few minutes telling each other what romance means to you. You might hear something important that you've missed before.

JCD

Out with the Garbage and Flannel Pajamas

My lover is mine and I am his.
Song of Songs 2:16

Were you surprised by the definition of romance your spouse offered last night? Romance can mean vastly different things to women and men, but for most of us the word describes that wonderful feeling of being noticed, wanted, and pursued—of being at the very center of our lover's attention. Women are inclined to define romance as the things a husband does to make them feel loved, protected, and respected. Flowers (if they aren't too cheap), compliments, nonsexual touching, and love notes are all steps in the right direction. So is helping with the chores. As author Kevin Leman once said, "The greatest of all aphrodisiacs is for a man to take out the garbage for his wife."

Men, on the other hand, rely more on their senses. They appreciate a wife who makes herself as attractive to her husband as possible. A man wants to be respected—and even better, admired—by his wife. He likes to hear his wife express genuine interest in his opinions, hobbies, and work.

Obviously, these are generalizations, so take your spouse's definition to heart. Knowing how he or she perceives romance can help you avoid many misunderstandings and disappointments. With a little care and forethought, you can keep the flame of romance burning brightly.

Just between us...

- What's the most romantic thing I've ever done for you?
- How do you feel about our personal definitions of romance?
- How can our differing views of romance strengthen our marriage?

Dear God, thank You for making us unique as a man and woman. Please help us understand and celebrate our carefully crafted differences. We want to become experts at pursuing and cherishing each other. Amen.

THE MYSTERY OF ROMANCE

Many waters cannot quench love; rivers cannot wash it away.
Song of Songs 8:7

No matter how hard we try to define romance, it remains in part a mystery. Yet Solomon's Song of Songs does give us several clues to its nature. In this evocative description of romantic love, we see that it means both intimacy and intense emotional excitement: "My lover is mine and I am his" (2:16); "My heart began to pound for him" (5:4). We see how deep affection inspires desire and complete appreciation for another: "How beautiful you are, my darling!" (4:1). We learn that to be romantic means to pursue the object of our affection—and to pine when he or she eludes us: "All night long on my bed I looked for the one my heart loves; I looked for him but did not find him" (3:1). And we see how powerfully a public display of affection communicates romantic love: "He has taken me to the banquet hall, and his banner over me is love" (2:4).

Most important of all, we learn that God intended romance to culminate in the unbreakable bond of married love. The book of Songs reaches its climax with a description of the power of love: "Love is as strong as death, its jealousy unyielding as the grave. It burns like a blazing fire, like a mighty flame" (8:6). The Lord would not have provided us with this scriptural celebration of love and romance unless He intended it as an inspiring example for us.

Just between us...

- How does Song of Songs demonstrate the importance of romance?
- How can romance encourage love "like a mighty flame"?
- In light of today's reading, would you alter your definition of romance in any way?

Heavenly Father, thank You for the blessing of romantic attraction. May my spouse and I pursue each other joyfully and creatively all of our days. Amen.

A TIME TO BE SILENT

There is a time for everything…
a time to be silent and a time to speak.
Ecclesiastes 3:1, 7

J(JCD) still remember the day, just two weeks before Shirley and I were married, when we proudly drove off a used car lot in the gleaming white 1957 Ford sedan I had just purchased. Five blocks down the road, to celebrate this historic event, I leaned over to give Shirley a quick kiss.

It wasn't quick enough! At that instant two cars in front of us made an unexpected stop. I crashed into the first and knocked it into a second. The front of my gorgeous car crumpled like an accordion. Fortunately, there were no injuries, except to my pride.

Because of this stupid mistake, I couldn't afford to buy Shirley a wedding ring with even a small diamond, and the car we had dreamed of buying for so long was severely damaged. Yet Shirley never let the accident tarnish the romantic aura of our early days together. I never heard a word of criticism about it, and on our first anniversary, I bought her the diamond ring. Forty years later, Shirley still hasn't complained about my bad driving!

We urge you to think before you say hurtful and unkind words that will burn in the memory of your spouse for many years. Protect your romantic relationship, even when criticism seems justified. Your love for each other is a precious and fragile flower. Treat it that way.

Just between us…

- Do we actively protect the element of romance in our marriage?
- Are we wise enough to know when it is "time to be silent"?
- When life's misfortunes strike, is there still a feeling of romance between us?

Lord, You ask us to keep our marriage partner's interests uppermost in our minds, but sometimes this doesn't come naturally. Help us to be more thoughtful, giving, and forgiving in how we tend each other's hearts. Amen.

OLD HAUNTS, NEW MEMORIES

*Praise the Lord...who satisfies your desires with good
things so that your youth is renewed like the eagle's.*
Psalm 103:2, 5

*S*hirley and I celebrated our wedding anniversary a few years
ago by exploring what we called our "old haunts." We took
an entire day together, beginning with a visit to the Farmer's
Market, where we had strolled as young lovers. Then we had a leisurely
lunch at a favorite restaurant and talked of things long ago. Afterwards we
saw a theater performance at the Pasadena Playhouse, where we had gone
on our second date, and later we had cherry pie and coffee at Gwinn's
Restaurant, a favorite hangout for dating couples. We talked about our
warm memories and relived the excitement of earlier days. It was a wonderful reprise.

If your marriage feels stagnant, maybe it's time to experience again
the wonderful places and events from your courtship or newlywed days.
Re-create your first date. Walk the same stretch of beach or mountain trail
you used to enjoy. Return to the place you got engaged. Visit the church
or chapel where you were married. Drive by the house or apartment
where you first lived. Sing the old songs. Tell the old stories.

I think you'll find that the old thrill is still there waiting for you.

Just between us...

- What were our favorite places to go, or things to do, during our
  courtship?
- Which of our dates or outings would you most like to re-create?
- How can we make sure we have experiences now that we'll look back
  on with fondness?

*Lord, thank You so much for the good old days of courtship. Help us to make
many new ones in the days ahead. Amen.*

"ORDINARY" LOVE

Live a life of love, just as Christ loved us.

Ephesians 5:2

We've been talking about romantic love and how to preserve it. There are times in every marriage, however, when husbands and wives feel apathetic and "flat" toward each other. Jim wrote me the following note during just such a time, which occured on our eighth wedding anniversary:

"I'm sure you remember the many occasions during our eight years of marriage when the tide of love and affection soared high above the crest. This kind of intense emotion often accompanies a time of particular happiness. We felt this closeness when the world's most precious child came home from the maternity ward. But emotions are strange! We felt the same closeness when you were hospitalized last year. I felt it intensely when I knelt over your unconscious form after a grinding automobile accident.

"Both happiness and threat bring overwhelming appreciation and affection for our sweethearts. But most of life is composed of calm, everyday events. During those times, I enjoy the serene love that actually surpasses the effervescent display. I find myself in that kind of love on this anniversary. I feel the steady, quiet affection that comes from a devoted heart. I am committed to you and your happiness now more than ever.

"When events throw us together emotionally, we will enjoy the thrill and romantic excitement. But during life's routine, my love stands undiminished. Happy anniversary to my wonderful wife."

Just between us...

- When has our marriage provided the most romantic excitement?
- How can serene love enhance romance between us?
- Do we enjoy this kind of love? Why or why not?

Dear God, thank You for the intense feelings that accompany romantic love. Help us cherish them. May our love also remain strong and enduring on ordinary days or when feelings are at ebb tide. Amen.

Just the Two of Us

Take me away with you—let us hurry!
Song of Songs 1:4

*W*hen Jim and I were dating, I was pleased to discover his creative, romantic side. Little things he did, such as sending me a love note hidden in a Coke bottle, made me feel special. I treasured those romantic moments from our early days together.

After we were married, we were extremely busy—Jim was finishing graduate training and I was teaching school. But we were still able to set aside an occasional weekend for just the two of us. We would wander through department stores, holding hands, laughing, and talking. We loved to window-shop for furniture and dream about how we hoped to decorate our house of the future. We would enjoy a light breakfast and then plan a candlelit dinner somewhere for the evening.

Life became even more hectic in the coming years, as God blessed our efforts in His service. We came to a point where we desperately needed some time alone. We arranged for my mother to keep the kids, and we drove six hours north to a winter wonderland called Mammoth, California. That weekend turned out to be a highlight of our marriage. I felt like a college girl again. We talked along the way and stopped to eat whenever it suited our fancy. The next morning we donned our ski clothes and headed for a wonderful restaurant, The Swiss Café. Hilda, the bubbly Swedish lady who owned the restaurant, called me "Shoooolie."

Our conversation at the breakfast table took us back into each other's worlds. Jim's eyes never looked bluer, and the love that's always there between us, steady and committed, surged to an emotional peak.

Driving to the ski lodge was equally exhilarating. The roads looked like a Christmas card. The giant evergreens appeared majestic in their white fur coats. I knew it was going to be a great day for skiing. Once on the mountain, we swished back and forth across the slopes like two adolescents.

We were wonderfully exhausted driving back to the condo. Jim prepared a cozy fire in the fireplace while I made our favorite meal of fried burritos. We ate dinner by the firelight, discussing our day and an endless variety of topics. After the dinner dishes were cleaned up, we pulled the pillows off the couch, chose some of our favorite records, and put them on the stereo. We relaxed in front of the fire and talked for hours. We also agreed to try to repeat our private rendezvous at least once a year. The memories of that weekend motivated me for many days to be the wife and mother I needed to be.

Is it time for you to take a similar romantic trip? Even if finances are tight, just being together can rekindle "that lovin' feeling." All that is needed is a little effort and creative flair. Talk with your mate; ask him or her what would bring new interest and excitement to your marriage. Then schedule at least two "getaway" activities a month when you can be alone together. If you keep the fire of your relationship well tended with romance, you'll enjoy its warmth throughout your marriage.

SMD

The Gift of Sex

A GENTLE CARESS

by Daphna Renan

ichael and I hardly noticed when the waitress came and placed the plates on our table. We were seated in a small deli tucked away from the bustle of Third Street in New York City. Even the smell of our recently arrived blintzes was no challenge to our excited chatter. In fact, the blintzes remained slumped in their sour cream for quite some time. We were enjoying ourselves too much to eat.

Our exchange was lively, if not profound. We laughed about the movie that we had seen the night before and disagreed about the meaning behind the text we had just finished for our literature seminar. He told me about the moment he had taken a drastic step into maturity by becoming Michael and refusing to respond to "Mikey." Had he been twelve or fourteen? He couldn't remember, but he did recall that his mother had cried and said he was growing up too quickly. As we finally bit into our blueberry blintzes, I told him about the blueberries that my sister and I used to pick when we went to visit our cousins in the country. I recalled that I always finished mine before we got back to the house, and my aunt would warn me that I was going to get a bad stomachache. Of course, I never did.

As our sweet conversation continued, my eyes glanced across the restaurant, stopping at the small corner booth where an elderly couple sat. The woman's floral-print dress seemed as faded as the cushion on which she had rested her worn handbag. The top of the man's head was as shiny as the soft-boiled egg he slowly nibbled. She also ate her oatmeal at a slow, almost tedious pace.

But what drew my thoughts to them was their undisturbed silence. It seemed to me that a melancholy emptiness permeated their little corner. As the exchange between Michael and me fluctuated from laughs to whispers, confessions to assessments, this couple's poignant stillness called to me. How sad, I thought, not to have anything left to say. Wasn't there any page that they hadn't yet turned in each other's stories? What if that happened to us?

Michael and I paid our small tab and got up to leave the restaurant. As we walked by the corner where the old couple sat, I accidentally dropped my wallet. Bending over to pick it up, I noticed that under the table, each of their free hands was gently cradled in the other's. They had been holding hands all this time!

I stood up feeling humbled by the simple yet profound act of connection I had just been privileged to witness. This man's gentle caress of his wife's tired fingers filled not only what I had previously perceived as an emotionally empty corner, but also my heart. Theirs was not the uncomfortable silence that threatens to fill the space after the punch line or at the end of an anecdote on a first date. No, theirs was a comfortable, relaxed ease, a gentle love that did not always need words to express itself. They had probably shared this hour of the morning with each other for a long time, and maybe today wasn't that different from yesterday, but they were at peace with that—and with each other.

Maybe, I thought as Michael and I walked out, it wouldn't be so bad if someday that was us. Maybe it would be kind of nice.

LOOKING AHEAD...

When husband and wife have achieved true intimacy, like the elderly couple holding hands in tonight's story, they can enjoy and appreciate each other at the deepest level. That's true at the corner deli and in the bedroom.

Some would say that "having sex" and "making love" are one and the same, but there's an important distinction between the two. The physical act of intercourse can be accomplished by any appropriately matched mammals, as well as most other members of the animal kingdom. But the art of making love, as designed by God, is a much more meaningful and complex experience—it's physical, emotional, and spiritual. In marriage we should settle for nothing less than a sexual relationship that is expressed not only body to body, but heart to heart and soul to soul.

As we discuss this subject in the days ahead, you and your partner may want to ask each other: Is our physical intimacy all that it could be?

JCD

WHAT'S YOUR MOTIVE?

I belong to my lover, and his desire is for me.
Song of Songs 7:10

L et's face it: Sex is a topic on the mind of just about every husband and wife. (Some wives claim their husbands think of
nothing else!) The physical union of man and woman is one
of the most pleasurable and meaningful aspects of marriage. Yet when a
couple engages in sex for the wrong reasons, intercourse quickly loses its
significance and can become an empty obligation. The late Dr. David
Hernandez once offered some common, "nonloving" motives for sex:

- to fulfill one's marital duty,
- to repay or secure a favor,
- as a conquest,
- as a substitute for verbal communication,
- to overcome feelings of inferiority,
- as an enticement for emotional love,
- as a defense against anxiety and tension,
- as a form of self-gratification without seeking to satisfy the other.

God designed sex as an intimate expression of love between husband
and wife. Anything that fails to meet that standard leaves one partner feeling unsatisfied and exploited.

Just between us...

- When was the last time you thought about making love?
- Does your motive for sex ever fall into any of the above categories?
- Have you ever felt sexually "used" by me?
- How can we move from "having sex" toward "making love"?

*Heavenly Father, You have blessed our union with sexual expression. Bless us
with emotional and sexual intimacy as well. Thank You for the pleasure and
wonder of married lovemaking. Amen.*

TWO SIDES OF PASSION

*The wife's body does not belong to her alone but also to
her husband. In the same way, her husband's body
does not belong to him alone but also to his wife.*

1 Corinthians 7:4

*T*here's a basic difference between women and men that marriage partners need to understand: Women tend to give sex to get intimacy, while men tend to give intimacy to get sex. Many men, for example, can separate the act of intercourse from the relationship and feel some measure of physical satisfaction. Not so for most women. More relationally inclined, they often feel exploited when sexual relations are not accompanied by tenderness, caring, and romantic love.

Solutions? The man who wants an exciting sexual experience with his wife should focus on the other twenty-three and a half hours in the day. He should compliment her, tell her that he cares, and make her feel special in a hundred different ways. Turning the coin over, the wife must understand that her husband is more visually oriented and easily stimulated than she is. She should make herself as attractive to him as she can.

With a little unselfish forethought, each can learn to satisfy the other. In our experience, responding to these basic differences opens the door for genuine passion in marriage.

Just between us...

- Do you agree that men and women approach sex differently?
- Do we understand each other's feelings about sex and intimacy?
- Why do you think God created these differences in men and women?
- What can I do specifically to make sex more appealing to you?

*Lord, help us to hold our differences about sexual attraction in high regard—
never hindering where we could help, never ignoring or criticizing where we
could cherish and honor. Thank You that we can give ourselves to each other
so completely. Amen.*

TWELVE-STEP BONDING

Above all, love each other deeply.
1 Peter 4:8

*D*o you feel "bonded" to your mate? Bonding refers to the emotional connectedness that links a man and woman together for life and makes them irreplaceable to each other. It is God's gift of closest companionship to those who have experienced it.

According to Drs. Donald Joy and Desmond Morris, bonding is most likely to occur between those who have moved systematically and slowly through the following twelve steps during their courtship and marriage: 1) Eye to body. 2) Eye to eye. 3) Voice to voice. 4) Hand to hand. 5) Hand to shoulder. 6) Hand to waist. 7) Face to face. 8) Hand to head. 9) Hand to body. 10) Mouth to breast. 11) Touching below the waist. 12) Intercourse. The final acts of physical contact should, of course, be reserved for the marital relationship.

In the most successful unions, husbands and wives journey through each of the twelve steps regularly. Touching, talking, holding hands, and gazing into one another's eyes are as important to partners in their midlife years as to twenty-year-olds. Indeed, the best way to reinvigorate a tired sex life is to walk through the twelve steps of courtship frequently and with gusto!

Just between us...

- During our courtship, did we follow this progression of bonding steps?
- Are we regularly experiencing each level of bonding now?
- How can we strengthen our physical and emotional bonding in our relationship?

Dear Father, if we have been careless in the different kinds of relational bonding, forgive us. Help us to become one in body and soul. Amen.

Newlywed Nonsense

"Where is the respect due me?"
Malachi 1:6

ome years ago as I (JCD) was flipping through the TV channels, I paused momentarily to watch a "newlywed" show. It was a bad decision. The host posed a series of dumb questions to a lineup of brides whose husbands were "sequestered backstage in a soundproof room."

The host challenged the women to predict their husband's responses to inquiries that went something like this: "Using the TV terms 'first run,' 'rerun,' or 'cancelled,' how would you describe the first time you and your husband made 'whoopee'?" Without the least hesitation, the women blurted out frank answers to this and other intimate questions. A few minutes later the men were given the same opportunity to humiliate their wives. Of course, they grabbed it.

It has been said that television programming reflects the values of the society it serves. Heaven help us if that is true. In this instance, the newlyweds revealed their immaturity, selfishness, hostility, vulnerability, and sense of inadequacy. Rather than treat their sexual relationships—and each other—with the privacy and respect they deserved, these young marrieds aired every intimate detail to a national television audience without a second thought.

Intimacy will never be achieved in the bedroom, or in any part of the marriage, when the relationship is handled in so cavalier a manner. Some facts about your life together are best kept between you and your mate.

Just between us...

- Do you feel I respect our sexual relationship?
- Do I ever reveal details about our sex life you wish I didn't?
- How can the behavior described above damage a relationship?

Lord, thank You for the intimacy that we share. May we be quick to recognize and reject popular values that offend You and our marriage commitment. Amen.

GOD'S GIFT

The man and his wife were both naked, and they felt no shame.

Genesis 2:25

*I*n previous generations, some people believed women were not supposed to enjoy sex. Even today some Christians still feel that sex between marital partners is somehow sinful or "dirty." But there's nothing biblical about either viewpoint.

The Lord created us as sexual beings and gave us the gift of physical intimacy as a means for expressing love between husband and wife. In the biblical account of the Garden of Eden, we are told that "a man will leave his father and mother and be united to his wife, and they will become one flesh." The Bible says that before sin entered the picture, the first husband and wife were unashamed of their nakedness (Genesis 2:24–25).

Scripture also uses sexual symbolism to describe the relationship between God and man. (Look, for example, at Isaiah 62:5; Jeremiah 7:9 and 23:10; Ezekiel 16; Hosea; Ephesians 5; and Revelation 19:6–7.) In addition, Solomon's Song of Songs clearly celebrates sexual pleasure between married lovers. We suggest that you set time aside to read that book together.

As designed by God, sexual desire in marriage is more than an afterthought or a means to guarantee procreation. That's why we can wholeheartedly say, "Let's 'make love' the way our God intended!"

Just between us...

- While growing up, did you receive positive or negative messages about sex? How do you think this has affected our love life?
- Do you think of sex as a gift from God?
- Is there anything about our love life that you'd like to tell me?

Dear God, thank You for making Your wonderful intentions for married sex so clear in Scripture. Where we have trampled on this gift, forgive us. We want so much to "make love" Your way. Amen.

GOD'S RECIPE FOR SEX

Let my lover come into his garden
and taste its choice fruits.
Song of Songs 4:16

*S*omeone once said that in matters of sex, men are like microwaves and women are like crockpots. There is certainly some truth to that cooking analogy—husbands can reach their "boiling point" before many wives have even decided what's on the menu!

Why would God make men and women this way? Don't our different makeups set us up for conflict when our attention turns to physical intimacy?

I believe the Lord knew just what He was doing when He established these fundamental differences between us. After all, if women were more like men, we'd all probably spend so much time in the bedroom that we'd never get anything else done. And if men were more like women, we'd enjoy many more meaningful conversations—but the species might just disappear!

Our differences are what make life so interesting and invigorating. They force us to reach out, to grow, to appreciate our partner. When a husband is extroverted and the wife is introverted, the husband draws out the wife, while the wife helps the husband take time to reflect. When a wife is spontaneous and her husband is a planner, she brings energy and excitement to his life, while he adds stability to hers.

So it is with sex. Emotional and physical differences create interest and excitement. We encourage you to celebrate them! After all, when marital partners are joined as "one flesh," it is more than a physical union. We are merging our whole beings—body, mind, and spirit—in a wonderful and sacred encounter. This is just what your loving God intended. You can enjoy the variety that each of you brings to your marriage—no matter what you're cooking.

SMD

How Trust Happens

DREAM LOVER

by Patrick O'Neill

*T*he clock radio was playing a gentle tune, and I woke up to another day of infinite wonder and promise.

"Morning, sweetie," I said, my head still snuggled in my pillow.

"Who's Angela?" my wife asked me in the tone Mike Wallace uses when cameras are chasing some poor jerk down a sidewalk in Newark, New Jersey.

Thousands of years of evolving and adapting have given married men a kind of sixth sense that tells them when to be absolutely truthful, answering all questions fully and without reservation.

"I don't know any Angela," I said.

"Oh, I know you don't," Kathleen said, sitting up and slamming her hand on the alarm button. "This is so ridiculous. It's just that I had this dream last night, and in it you left me and the kids and ran off with some Angela woman. I've been awake for three hours getting madder and madder."

"Silly girl," I said, snuggling deeper into the blankets. "I promise I didn't run off with anybody. Not last night or any other night. And especially not with any Angela."

Kathleen threw back the blankets with considerably more force than the circumstances required and got out of bed.

"It was just a dream," I said, wishing desperately for two more minutes of unconsciousness. "I don't know an Angela. I'm here with you and our children. I'm not leaving. Never, ever."

The shower door banged shut, and I drifted off. Suddenly a wet towel hit me in the face.

"Sorry, hon, I was aiming for the hamper," Kathleen said. "Anyway, you and Angela were living together in one of those luxury high-rise condos downtown."

"Ha. See how crazy that is? Child support would wipe me out. I couldn't afford to live under a bridge if I left you. Which I have no plans to do."

"Angela's a surgeon," she said as if she were talking to a complete idiot. "With an international reputation. She's filthy rich. Or don't you realize that either? Oh, of course you don't. Just a dream."

"Listen, I know dreams can seem pretty realistic sometimes. But you're the woman of my dreams. Okay? What kind of surgeon?"

From the bathroom came the unmistakable sound of toiletries being destroyed.

"You want to know what really got me?" she said. "The kids. The kids went to visit one weekend, and you know what that—you know—Angela did? She made teddy bear pancakes. With little raisin eyes. The children talked about those for days: 'How come you never make us teddy bear pancakes, Mom?'"

"Teddy bear pancakes? That sounds kind of cute. They'd probably be pretty easy...."

"Oooooh," Kathleen said. "This is so dumb. How can anybody get upset over a stupid dream about her husband running off with a world-famous surgeon who can sit down at a piano with the kids and play all the television theme songs by ear and knows all the verses and can put your daughter's hair up in a perfect French braid and show your boy how to play 'stretch' with a jackknife and teach aerobics?"

"Kathleen, I couldn't love a surgeon. Surgeons are notoriously self-centered and egotistical. But maybe Angela was different."

"Angela works among the poor," Kathleen said. "Here's that tennis shoe you've been looking for.... Oops, are you all right? Anyway, the president gave her some kind of plaque. I saw it on TV. In my dream. There she was with those cheekbones and that mane of black hair. 'Others deserve this far more than I do, Mr. President.' I just about threw up."

The tennis shoe bruise probably wouldn't show unless I went swimming or something.

"What with teddy bear pancakes, humanitarianism, and piano lessons,

Angela couldn't have much time left over for a guy," I said. "I mean, a guy like me."

"Oh, no. The kids told me how she spent hours rubbing your shoulders, and sometimes she sat at your feet on that spotless white carpet—'It's like snow, Mom'—and stared up at you, laughing at every stupid little thing you said. Darn! Your watch fell in the sink. Sorry, sweetie."

"I think you're being a little hard on Angela," I said. "She sounds like a pretty nice person who's only trying to make a life for herself."

"She's a vicious little home wrecker, and if you ever so much as look at her again, you'll need more than a world-renowned surgeon to put you back together again!"

Later that day, I sent flowers to Kathleen's office. It's just a start, of course. When somebody like Angela comes into your life, it takes a while to patch things up.

LOOKING AHEAD...

Most married partners can admit it: At one time or another we have felt some anxiety about our spouse's commitment, whether because of a serious threat to the relationship or just a dream like Kathleen's.

Underneath the humor of Kathleen's "anxiety dream" is a very real issue—to trust or not to trust. The uncertainty many feel about trust is, unfortunately, a sign of the times. Infidelity and straying affections are far too common, and in some circles they are even accepted as inevitable. As Christians, we know that we can place unequivocal confidence in the Lord. But absolute, unquestioned trust in our spouse? That can be harder to bestow. The truth is, it must be earned over time—word by word, deed by deed.

Relationships dominated by fear and insecurity will never reach their potential, but marriages founded on trust and safety will flourish. You can see why it is so important for married couples to commit themselves to build trust together. In the week ahead we'll help you understand how trust happens and how to make it the bedrock of a secure and growing relationship.

JCD

GO STRAIGHT HOME

*Your enemy the devil prowls around like a
roaring lion looking for someone to devour.*

1 Peter 5:8

One of the great fears of many husbands and wives is that their partner will be unfaithful—an understandable concern, considering that nearly half of American marriages end in divorce, many because of infidelity. We must always be alert for Satan's attacks on marriage.

I (JCD) remember one trap in particular that the enemy laid for me. Shirley and I had been married just a few years when we had a minor spat. I got in the car and drove around for an hour to cool off. As I was on my way home, a very attractive girl drove up beside me and smiled. She was obviously flirting with me. She slowed down, looked back, and turned onto a side street. I knew she was inviting me to follow her.

I didn't take the bait; I went straight home and made up with Shirley. But I thought later about how quickly Satan had taken advantage of our conflict and my momentary vulnerability. That's how he operates. Expect him to lay a trap for you, too. Just make sure your partner can count on you to come home when temptation drives up.

Just between us...

- What does God's Word say about adultery? (We encourage you to take the time to review Exodus 20:14; Leviticus 18:20; 20:10; Proverbs 7; Malachi 3:5; Matthew 5:27–28; Mark 10:11–12; John 8:1–11; Romans 7:2–3; Ephesians 5:3–5; and Hebrews 13:4.)
- What does God promise regarding temptation (1 Corinthians 10:13)?
- How can we "affair proof" our marriage?

Lord, please give us wisdom and strength as we seek to affair-proof our marriage. Thank You for promising us a "way of escape" from temptation. Amen.

SAFETY RULES

Can a man walk on hot coals without his feet being scorched?
Proverbs 6:28

The surest way to avoid an affair is to flee temptation as soon as it confronts you. Author Jerry Jenkins has referred to this determination to preserve moral purity as "building hedges" around marriage so that temptation is never given a foothold. You take steps to protect yourself and enhance the trust level in your marriage at the same time.

How? Talk with your partner about your interactions with the opposite sex, then establish sensible, sensitive guidelines. Some couples rule out lunch with a coworker, traveling together, talking alone behind closed doors, sharing rides, or working as a "couple" on a project. Agree on what you both consider reasonable, then stick to that agreement. If you're faced with a situation that you haven't discussed, ask your spouse about it beforehand, and if he or she isn't comfortable with it, don't do it. *Listen* to each other's concerns. The Lord has made you "one flesh" for good reason.

At first it may seem strange to ask for permission to take part in what's probably a completely innocent activity. But you'll quickly discover how wonderfully reassuring it feels when the situation is reversed and your partner is the one asking you!

Just between us...

- Are you comfortable with my behavior around members of the opposite sex? Is there anything I should do differently?
- Are we praying enough that God would protect us from temptation?
- What does Proverbs 6:28 mean to you?

Dear God, we want to protect our marriage from any threat. We want to live freely and securely as a result of having chosen to live wisely. By Your Spirit, show us how to honor each other and please You. Amen.

ACTIONS EARN TRUST

If you think you are standing firm,
be careful that you don't fall!
1 Corinthians 10:12

*T*he surest way to build trust in marriage is through your actions. Build a record of choices and deeds that proves to your partner you can be trusted at all times.

Take flirting, for example. It may be harmless to show a bit of extra friendliness to a member of the opposite sex. But ask yourself, *Would my spouse feel comfortable if he or she witnessed this exchange? Would my actions earn trust, or would they raise doubt about my motives?*

I (JCD) urge you to be wary of pride in your own infallibility. The minute you begin thinking that an affair "would never happen to me" is when you become most vulnerable. We are sexual creatures with powerful urges. We are also fallen beings with strong desires to do wrong. That is what temptation is all about. Do *not* give it a place in your life. My father once wrote, "Strong desire is like a powerful river. As long as it stays within the banks of God's will, all will be proper and clean. But when it overflows those boundaries, devastation awaits downstream."

Actions can affect trust in easy-to-overlook ways. When you promise to clean out the garage next weekend, make sure you do it. When you agree to limit your spending to a certain amount, follow through. Keeping your word in small matters builds trust in a big way.

Just between us...

- Where is the line between friendly interest and flirting?
- What actions do I take that help you trust me?
- How did Jesus establish trust with His disciples?

Lord Jesus, thank You for being our example of trustworthiness and integrity. Help us every day to turn away from temptation and compromise. We want to be true in our innermost being. Amen.

HEALING WORDS

The tongue that brings healing is a tree of life.
Proverbs 15:4

o you enjoy teasing your wife? When you're with friends, do you occasionally reveal an embarrassing secret about your husband?

One key to building trust is to take great care not to hurt or embarrass those we love. Some information is private and should remain so. For one partner to reveal family secrets indiscriminately breaks the couple's bond of loyalty and violates trust.

Just as important as the words we don't say, however, are those we do. Men, especially, are often reluctant to share feelings and fears with their wives, yet openness fosters trust and intimacy. Sharing thoughts is vital to a healthy, secure marriage. How can a wife feel safe or valued if she's left guessing about what her husband is really thinking and feeling?

Along the same lines, if you're in charge of the family finances, and you've accidentally or foolishly depleted the bank account, don't hide it—let your spouse know. If someone makes a pass at you at work, tell your partner, even if it's uncomfortable to do so. As you work together to find the best solution for problems like these, you'll grow closer.

Just between us...

* Are you comfortable with the amount and nature of teasing in our relationship?
* Do I share my thoughts with you as much as you'd like?
* Do our words "bring healing" to each other?
* How can I help you share your feelings?

Dear God, let the words of our mouths always be true and full of grace. May our words bring healing and encouragement and draw us closer together. Amen.

Best Friends

A friend loves at all times.
Proverbs 17:17

There is a limit to the openness we have described. It can be used to create insecurity and gain power over your spouse. I (JCD) know of a handsome young company president who told his wife every day about the single women at the office who flirted with him. His candor was admirable, but by not *also* stressing his commitment to his wife, he was saying (consciously or not): "You'd better treat me right because there are plenty of women out there just waiting to get their hands on me." His wife began to fret about how she would hang onto her husband.

He should have reflected on his real motives for alarming his wife. Did this kind of sharing nurture or injure his friendship with her? And she could have helped redirect the conversations by pointing out to her husband—in a calm, nonthreatening manner—how his words made her feel.

If you reveal your inner feelings honestly, with pure motives, and continually reaffirm your commitment to your marriage, your spouse will become your most treasured confidante, protector, adviser, and friend. After forty years of marriage, I can happily report that Shirley and I are best, intimate friends—in no small part because we've earned each other's trust.

Just between us...

- Have you shown me the "real" you?
- How should we respond when our partner shares a weakness?
- How can I be a better friend?

Father, thank You so much that my spouse and I are lifetime partners. But we want to always be best and dearest friends, too. Bless us with Your wisdom, grace, and power to this end, we pray. Amen.

THE HOUSE THAT TRUST BUILT

Let love and faithfulness never leave you.
Proverbs 3:3

We've been talking this week about building trust—one of the essential components of a successful marriage. It's a bit like constructing a small house out of dominos. As you carefully lay them in place, each succeeding level depends on the previous one. The placement of each domino matters. If one is placed at an angle, the entire project will eventually come crashing down.

So it is with trust. Every aspect of marriage is connected. As we seek and follow God's will for our lives, we behave in ways that earn trust from our husband or wife. As that trust grows, our mate becomes more open and vulnerable to us. As we share more of ourselves with each other, we achieve greater intimacy, which makes us more accountable to our partners and provides a better setting for encouraging each other in our spiritual lives.

One night in college I decided to tell Jim about my painful past—that my father was an abusive alcoholic. We had gone together for about a year before I revealed this secret. I didn't know how Jim would react or if I could trust him with it. Actually, I was afraid the revelation might end our relationship. But as I talked, Jim put his arms around me and listened for a long time. When I was through, he told me that he had a new appreciation for me and for the strength I needed to live through such trying circumstances. Instead of driving us apart, my openness brought us closer together.

Clearly, you have to be very careful when choosing to share your intimate secrets. Some people will reject or hurt you or betray your confidence with others. However, one of the wonderful characteristics of love is that in a mature relationship, sharing leads to even greater trust. I hope that our conversations this week have already led you to a deeper experience of trust and confidence in each other.

SMD

Honor Your Mate

SURPRISE PARTY

by Gary Smalley

*I*t was the eve of his graduation from a long, grueling master's degree program. After four years of intensive, full-time study, he was finally about to receive his diploma.

His wife planned a special party so many of their friends could come and help him celebrate the long-awaited "day of deliverance." There would be cake, refreshments, banners, streamers, swimming, croquet, and other yard games. Many people had already accepted her invitation to attend, and it looked like it would be a full house. Her husband, though, had other ideas. He secretly contacted each person who had received an invitation and revealed his plan to make the party a surprise in honor of her. Yes, there would be banners, streamers, and all the rest, but they would bear her name, not his.

He wanted to do something special to let her know how much he appreciated the years of sacrifice she had devoted to his goal. Working full-time to put him through school and delaying her dreams of a house and family had, in many ways, been harder on her than the long hours of study had been on him.

When the day arrived, she was busy with preparations and last-minute details, still convinced that all was going according to plan. He arranged to get her away from the party site, and while she was gone, he put up a huge banner with her name on it. During that time, all the guests arrived as well.

She returned to be greeted with a loud "SURPRISE!" When she realized what was going on, she could barely fight back the tears. Her husband asked a few people to share what they most appreciated about her. Then he stood before them and, with tender words of love and admiration, expressed his gratitude for all she had done for him. When he was through, everyone saluted her with a toast of iced tea.

The rest of the evening was a fun-filled fiesta of laughing, catching up with one another, water volleyball, yard games, and more food than anyone could eat. It was a celebration of an experience they had shared, and by commemorating it in a special way, this husband created a life-long, romantic memorial to his wife's love and dedication.

LOOKING AHEAD...

I love this example of a wise husband. He understood that he had reached his goal largely because of the sacrifice and cooperation of his wife. He also had the wisdom to seize a perfect opportunity to honor her publicly. Frankly, I did the same thing when I received my Ph.D. Shirley had sacrificed for seven long years to help me complete my training. She thought the party was for me, but forty guests helped me tell her that she was the one being honored. I presented her with a sterling silver coffee and tea service set, which she still displays in our living room. I knew a man who finished his doctorate just a few years later and said nothing about the support and assistance his wife had given him. She was very hurt.

To honor someone means to show respect—to give deserved recognition and appreciation to him or her. How thoughtful are you of your spouse? Do you actively seek ways to elevate your husband or wife before friends or family? Those are vitally important questions.

We'll talk this week about the importance of honor in marriage. Tonight, why don't you each express why you feel honored to be married to your mate?

JCD

UNSUNG HEROES

Yours, O LORD, is the kingdom....
Wealth and honor come from you.
1 Chronicles 29:11–12

s a society, we are inclined to honor heroes and high achievers. We award a Purple Heart to soldiers wounded in action. We admire All-Americans who excel in college football, basketball, or baseball. We celebrate winners of the Nobel Peace Prize. We applaud students who graduate magna cum laude. We fawn over movie stars at the Academy Awards.

But who takes time to honor the wives and husbands who diligently fulfill their responsibilities each day? Who cares about these unsung heroes who give of themselves, sacrificing for their children or caring for each other? Most often, the only cheering section for such couples is themselves—but when one partner doesn't seem to notice, it's pretty tough for the other to feel valued or motivated.

Scripture is clear regarding this matter. The apostle Paul says, "Honor one another above yourselves" (Romans 12:10). There's no better place to apply this verse than in your home—with the husband or wife sitting next to you.

Just between us...

- What do you think honoring each other means in the context of marriage?
- Do you feel "honored" by me? Do you know, without a doubt, that I hold you in highest esteem?
- When in our marriage have you most felt this way? When have you not?

Dear Lord, in our rush to admire and celebrate the achievements of others, help us to remember the loving life partner right beside us who most deserves our appreciation and respect. Open our eyes to simple but meaningful ways we can show honor. Amen.

TAKEN FOR GRANTED

Honor one another above yourselves.
Romans 12:10

*E*ach of us has a heartfelt need to be honored and respected. All too often, however, we take our spouses for granted at home. Is it any wonder that so many mothers hold down jobs in the workplace today? Many work for financial reasons, but some do so to find the recognition and praise they don't get from their mates. Could this also be why many men spend excessive hours at work—to receive from colleagues the accolades that they don't get at home?

Your partner is a jack-of-all-trades who brings a host of skills to your marriage: provider, short-order cook, nurse, counselor, financial planner, gardener, arbiter of sibling disputes, spiritual leader, comforter, and much more. We encourage you to show your appreciation for these talents and services. Tell your wife how much you enjoy her cooking. Send your husband to work with a note praising him for his good judgment with the family budget. In front of guests, compliment her taste in home decor and his wise guidance of the children.

If we don't make our mate feel honored and respected, we may find our partner looking for recognition somewhere else.

Just between us...

- What couple do we know who is an example to us of honoring each other?
- Do we honor each other well? What opportunities to bestow honor have we missed?
- Have we sought recognition elsewhere because we weren't receiving enough at home?

Heavenly Father, forgive us for any self-centeredness or lack of consideration in our marriage. Please teach us to make honoring our spouse a reflex action, not a begrudging afterthought. Amen.

GAMES PEOPLE PLAY

If anything is excellent or praiseworthy—
think about such things.
Philippians 4:8

*H*ave you ever been to a party and watched someone play "Assassinate the Spouse?" The objective is simple: A contestant attempts to punish his mate by ridiculing her in front of their friends. If he wants to be especially vicious, he lets the guests know he thinks she is dumb and ugly. It's a brutal game with no winners. The contest ends when his wife is totally divested of self-respect and dignity; he gets bonus points if he can reduce her to tears.

Sound cruel? It is, even when it's carried out under the guise of joking or teasing. It's never enjoyable to watch someone take out anger against his (or her) mate in this way. In contrast, what a pleasure it is to spend time with couples who continually build each other up in front of others. When a husband tells his guests about his wife's incredible cooking, patience with the kids, or promotion at work—or the wife boasts about her husband's talent on the job or his ability to speak in public or fix broken pipes—you'll see the other spouse smile a bit more brightly and stand a little taller. We're always most sensitive to the comments of our mate in the presence of our peers.

The next time you're out with friends, remember to look for opportunities to honor your mate. Leave the game playing to others.

Just between us...

- Have I embarrassed or hurt you in public? If so, can we talk about it?
- How do you feel when I praise you in front of our friends?
- In what ways could we build each other up in public?

Father, we want to show each other love, honor, and consideration always—but especially in front of others. Forgive us for our failures. Give us grace to learn and change, we pray. Amen.

Is Honor Overdue?

Humility comes before honor.
Proverbs 15:33

M r. Smith learned that his neighbor, Mr. Jones, had presented flowers and a gift to Mrs. Jones five nights in a row. He thought, *That must be what wins a woman's heart.* So Smith went out and bought a big box of candy and a bouquet of his wife's favorite flowers. Arriving home a little early that afternoon, he rang the doorbell. When Mrs. Smith appeared, he passionately embraced her. Suddenly she sagged and fell in a heap on the floor. "My goodness! What's wrong?" he exclaimed.

When she regained consciousness, she explained. "Oh, this has been the worst day! Our son received a terrible report card; Mother was admitted to the hospital; the roast burned; the washing machine broke. Now to top it off, you come home drunk!"

If your partner can't even fathom the possibility that you would bring her flowers or a gift (or some similar surprise), take the hint. It's time to work on honoring your mate!

Just between us...

* Would you be shocked if I brought you flowers or some other gift?
* What's the best surprise I ever gave you?
* What kind of thoughtful gesture would be enjoyable and honoring to you?
* Do you prefer being surprised in front of friends or in private?

Lord, we confess that the hurly-burly pace of living often threatens to suffocate our relationship. Remind us to care for each other. Help us to encourage others who are struggling in their marriages. Amen.

HONORING MOM AND DAD

"Honor your father and your mother."
Exodus 20:12

Who do you think is most responsible for establishing a child's opinion of his mother or father? The other parent, that's who! Each wields tremendous influence over what the children think of the other. Early in my marriage to Shirley, I learned that occasional irritation between us quickly reflected itself in the behavior of our kids. They seemed to think, *If Dad can argue with Mom, then we can, too.* In short, my attitude became the attitudes of my children. I realized how important it was to openly express love and admiration for my wife, even when there were issues that we needed to iron out in private.

If you're the father in the home, I encourage you to remind your kids how hard their mother works and how wonderful she is. And if you're the mother, praise your husband's courage and principles in front of the children. Kids will quickly recognize and mirror the respect fathers and mothers give each other. Showing honor now will pay off for years to come.

Just between us...

- How did your parents show respect to each other?
- Have we done a good job of honoring each other, and the Lord, in front of our children? In which situations are we most likely to fail?
- How could we improve?
- Do we know a couple that sets a good example in this area? What do they do that seems to really work?

Almighty God, we want to be good examples of honoring each other so that our children will grow up to honor their father and mother. We ask for Your wisdom and grace as we seek to excel in honoring one another in our home. Thank You for Your love. Amen.

A KING AND HIS QUEEN

"Those who honor me I will honor."
1 Samuel 2:30

can't think of a better example of honor between husband and wife than the biblical account of Queen Esther and Xerxes, king of Persia, in the book of Esther. The young queen was faced with a terrible dilemma: Her people, the Jews, were to be killed as part of a ruthless plot concocted by one of the king's most powerful nobles. Yet by law, no one, not even the queen, was allowed to approach the king without being summoned.

Esther relied on the principle of honor to protect her in this predicament. After fasting and, I'm sure, praying for three days, she went to the inner court of the palace. Rather than barging in, she waited patiently in the king's hall. When the king saw Esther, he invited her in. She showed further respect for Xerxes by touching his scepter when she arrived. When the king asked her why she had come, Esther did not answer immediately. Instead, she invited the king to a banquet she had prepared, thus paying further tribute to her husband. At the banquet, she invited the king to yet another banquet the next day. Only then did she finally make her request known.

Every time Esther addressed her husband, she conveyed sincere respect. She used phrases such as "if it pleases the king"; "if [the king] regards me with favor and thinks it the right thing to do"; and "if I have found favor with you, O king." Xerxes responded by honoring his wife— and granting her request! Through her courage and conduct, the Jews were spared a holocaust. In fact, King Xerxes went further: The evil noble was hanged, and the Jews were given new privileges and rights in the kingdom.

Our nature as humans is to criticize our spouse or complain about his or her shortcomings. Yet there is something attractive—and very compelling—about approaching each other as husband or wife with the deep respect and honor we would show royalty. I urge you to try approaching each other in just this way—even when you do not feel particularly close. Your reward will be a home environment that is more loving, positive, and enjoyable than you ever thought possible.

SMD

Choose Joy

MAY I HAVE THIS DANCE?

by Nancy Jo Sullivan

ordered a bag of popcorn at the snack bar while my girls scurried through the department store searching for Christmas gifts. I yawned as the clerk handed me my snack. I could barely keep my eyes open.

We had just moved into a new home. In between unpacking boxes, I had baked cookies, wrapped presents, and written cards of greeting.

So far the holidays had left me feeling depleted of energy. I wanted to feel close to God, especially in this season, but I hadn't had time for prayer and quiet reflection.

As I settled into a booth, I noticed an old man standing near the store entryway. Though his face was wrinkled, his eyes twinkled with the energy of youth. He was ringing a Salvation Army bell.

I watched as he danced around his red coin kettle, bobbing and turning to the rhythm of his own footsteps. Ringing his bell in carefully timed beats, he waved and smiled to those who passed him by.

"Joy to the world...mmm...the Lord is come."

Soon a woman made her way past the singing man. She was wearing a Christmas-tree sweater, her brow was furrowed, and she carried several shopping bags.

"No joy for the Lord?" the old man called out to her.

The woman sighed and rolled her eyes. She hurried to her car.

I watched as people hustled past the man. Most of them ignored him. Everyone seemed preoccupied with balancing their bags and boxes of presents.

A businessman with a cell phone walked past the dancing bell ringer. "Let every heart...mmm...Prepare him room..." the old man sang.

The sound of his bell and the beeping noise from the cash registers forced the businessman to shout into the phone. He reminded me of how all my seasonal obligations made me feel. I was trying to find a way to converse with God, but so far I hadn't gotten a good connection.

As busy shoppers made a wide perimeter around the bell ringer, an old woman, her back hunched and her gait slow, aproached him. She smiled as she clicked open a tattered purse and dropped four quarters into the slotted red pail.

The man took off his ear-muffed hat and bowed to her.

"May I have this dance?" he asked.

The woman blushed and began to giggle. As she drew herself up, her wrinkles seemed to fade. The two of them began to shuffle around the store entry, the old man gently guiding the frail woman in graceful glides and turns.

"Joy to the world...the Savior reigns..." their voices rang out in happy unison.

As I watched, I found myself wanting to join their department store waltz. Theirs was a dance of joy, unencumbered by stress or preoccupation—a dance of praise that proclaimed anew the tender message of old:

"Joy to the world...the Lord is come!"

Later that night, as my family slept upstairs, I curled up on the couch in our family room. After turning on my favorite holiday CD, I drank a cup of tea in front of our brightly lit tree. Soon the notes of "Joy to the World" filled the room.

I could almost hear the Lord say, "May I have this dance?"

LOOKING AHEAD...

Like the woman in the Christmas-tree sweater and the businessman with the cell phone, so few people seem to experience joy. No matter what time of year it is, they are preoccupied with the stress of the season and have either rejected or forgotten the joy that Jesus offers.

Yet none of us needs to live this way, for believers in the Lord know an eternal joy that ultimately transcends any hardship experienced in this world. Even in the midst of trials, He stands ready to lead us out of our suffering into His wonderful presence.

This next week we'll talk about how to choose joy in our marriages and in our lives. We *can* learn to rejoice and praise Him every day. The Lord has come!

JCD

ATTITUDE CONTROL

Your attitude should be the same as that of Jesus Christ.
Philippians 2:5

*O*ne morning, the late Bishop Fulton Sheen entered a greasy spoon for breakfast. "Bring me some ham and eggs and a few kind words for the day," he said.

The waitress returned fifteen minutes later and set the food before him. "There," she said.

"What about the kind words?" he asked.

She looked him over and replied, "I'd advise you not to eat them eggs!"

Sometimes the first few events of the day make it clear it's going to be a "downer." No matter what you do, you can't stop life's bad turns: the car that rear-ends yours on the way to work; the traffic jam that causes you to miss an important appointment. Yet you *can* choose your reaction to such irritating events.

We can live happily despite the ups and downs of everyday living, but to do so takes a great measure of dependence on Jesus Christ. The apostle Paul said it best: "I know what it is to be in need, and I know what it is to have plenty. I have learned the secret of being content in any and every situation, whether well fed or hungry, whether living in plenty or in want. I can do everything through Him who gives me strength." (Philippians 4:12–13).

Just between us...

- Am I generally cheerful and optimistic—or gloomy and pessimistic?
- How do I usually react when I'm disappointed or discouraged?
- How do my mood swings affect you and our marriage?
- How can we respond more positively to difficult events?

Dear Father, we invite You to be at work in us—individually and in our relationship—to grow in us the same attitude as Jesus Christ. We don't want to be ruled by circumstances or moods but by Your Spirit. Amen.

CHARLIE WEDEMEYER

Our present sufferings are not worth comparing
with the glory that will be revealed in us.
Romans 8:18

*L*ife was good for Charlie Wedemeyer. He was married to a beautiful woman, Lucy, had two wonderful children, and was a successful high school teacher and football coach. When he noticed a weakness in his hands, however, he visited a doctor. The doctor told him he had ALS (Lou Gehrig's disease), that in a few years he would be totally paralyzed, and that eventually he would die. Charlie's disease worsened in the years that followed. Time appeared to be running out. Then two things changed his life—he began using a portable respirator, and he became a Christian.

Today, more than twenty years after being diagnosed, Charlie and Lucy have touched thousands of lives during their appearances across the country. He cannot walk, speak, or even breathe on his own, but he chooses not to dwell on his infirmities.

"Pain and suffering are inescapable," Charlie says through Lucy's translation. "It's up to us to decide if we're going to be miserable or if we're going to try to make the most of our lives."

Charlie Wedemeyer is making the most of his. How about you?

Just between us...

- How would either of us respond if we faced a situation like Charlie's?
- So far in life, how much have we been asked to suffer?
- Who in the Bible suffered from disease or disability yet demonstrated trust in God? (For examples, see 2 Kings 5:1–14; 20:1–6; Matthew 9:27–29; Mark 5:25–29; 10:48–52; and 2 Corinthians 12:7–10.)

Father, thank You for promising to be with us when we suffer. Help us not to complain too much about life's little hurts, and help us to place our big sorrows in Your tender care. Amen.

The Trouble Paradox

*Carry each other's burdens, and in this
way you will fulfill the law of Christ.*
Galatians 6:2

hen troubles line up in what seems like an endless parade,
feelings of despair or helplessness can be overwhelming.
One way out of this downward spiral toward depression is
to reach out to someone else. Our own difficulties seem less threatening
and all-consuming when we are busy helping someone else handle
theirs.

The possibilities for helping others are limitless. Visit the sick. Bake
something for your neighbors. Do household chores for an elderly shut-in.
Use your car for those without transportation. And, perhaps most important, be a good listener. Sometimes what a person needs most of all is
simply a friend who will share his or her life for a few moments.

This is one of the powerful paradoxes of the Christian life: When we
share someone else's pain, we often shed some of our own. When we help
others, we end up helping ourselves. When we lift another's burdens, ours
lighten.

Just between us...

- What do you do when you're discouraged or depressed?
- Am I helpful to you when you're feeling down?
- In what ways did Jesus minister to the downhearted?
- Is there someone in a difficult situation who could use our help?

*Dear God, thank You for Your goodness during trouble. Increasingly, make us
Your instruments to help others in need. Help us to share Your comfort and
testify to Your great faithfulness. Thank You that we'll be blessed in doing so.
Amen.*

LEAVING "VICTIM" BEHIND

To this you were called, because Christ
suffered for you, leaving you an example.
1 Peter 2:21

*P*olitically correct notions in the culture today would lead us to believe that we all have reasons to be angry about the biases arrayed against us. The supposed discrimination extends to girls, boys, the elderly, homosexuals, drug addicts, alcoholics, atheists, those who are overweight, balding, short, undereducated, women (representing 51.2 percent of the population), and now, white men. There's hardly a person alive who doesn't have a claim against an oppressor in one context or another. I (JCD) call it "the victimization of everyone."

Unquestionably, there *are* disadvantaged people among us who need legal protection and special consideration, including some racial minorities. But the idea that the majority is exploited and disrespected is terribly destructive—first, because the belief that "they're out to get me" paralyzes us and leads to hopelessness and despair; second, because it divides people into separate and competing self-interest groups and pits them against each other.

The Scripture gives us a better way. It tells us to thank God every day for His blessings and to focus our attention not on ourselves, but on those who are less fortunate. Not once does it support or sanction the curse of victimization. Do not yield to it.

Just between us...

- Do we usually blame someone or something for our circumstances?
- How does playing the role of a victim make us tend to give up?
- What does God promise us for our earthly struggles?

Lord, forgive us for our quickness to shift into "victim thinking." Show us which hard things we can change and which we should accept as Your loving best for us. And grant us Your grace and joy in both circumstances. Amen.

WATCH OUT FOR TRAPS

Whoever believes in him shall not perish but have eternal life.
John 3:16

*W*e've found that retired couples and stay-at-home spouses are especially likely to fall into four traps that can take the joy out of life. Here they are, along with some suggestions for avoiding each trap.

First is the trap of *isolation*. Don't allow yourself to withdraw within your own four walls. Stay connected to people even when it's easier to stay home.

The second trap is *inactivity*. The simple act of taking a walk, visiting the library, or going grocery shopping keeps the muscles limber and the mind alert.

Third is the trap of *self-pity*. This attitude can cripple or even kill you! To ward it off, reach out to others. Develop a ministry of prayer and hospitality for those around you.

The fourth trap is *despair*. The elderly, in particular, can slip into thinking that life is over and no longer worth living. Yet the Christian must always be future oriented. The beauty of our faith lies in the assurance of the next world, where true joy awaits us all.

Just between us...

* Do you ever fall into any of these traps? Which one(s)?
* What specific things can we do to avoid them?
* Are you looking forward to the future? Why or why not?
* How does God use the elderly for His purposes?
* How could praying and caring for others lead to joy for us?

Father, we are so thankful that we will one day leave life's troubles behind and enter the joy of eternity with You. In the meantime, help us redeem the time for Your glory, confident that You are ready to work out Your divine purposes in every moment. Amen.

Our God of Joy

Rejoice in the Lord always.
I will say it again: Rejoice!
Philippians 4:4

The late entertainer Joe E. Brown once said, "I have no understanding of the long-faced Christian. If God is anything, He must be joy." How true! We have a God who loves us more than we love our children or even ourselves—a God who sent His Son to die for us and who has prepared a place in eternity just for us. He is indeed a God of joy—and we have much to be joyful about!

This is a lesson I had to learn the hard way. When we were first married, Jim and I taught school, served in the church, and carried many responsibilities. Jim was working on his master's degree at the time, so he wasn't able to help me carry my load. I looked forward every week to Saturday, when I could rest and recuperate. Gradually, I fell into the trap of being truly happy only one day a week. And if anything took that day away from me, I was very frustrated. Slowly, I learned to enjoy every day of the week, even though I was busy. It was a simple change in attitude that brightened my life. Someone once said, "If you have to cross the street to be happy, you're not seeing things properly." I agree.

There are many "long-faced" Christians who are caught up in the trials of this world. It's not always easy to remember that we can experience joy even in the midst of struggles. We forget that Jesus told us that our worldly grief would be like a mother giving birth: She experiences pain during labor, but then forgets her anguish because of her joy over the birth of her child (John 16:21). We forget that the apostles, after being flogged on orders of the Sanhedrin, left there "rejoicing because they had been counted worthy of suffering disgrace for the Name" (Acts 5:41).

Joy is something we experience when we begin to understand the magnitude of God and the love He freely gives us. It's not something to be grasped, but shared. It's not something to be contained, but made available to all. Joy is a selfless, abundant quality modeled by our Lord

Jesus. He is the one who has called us to "rejoice" and "leap for joy" when we are poor, hungry, weeping, hated, and rejected, because "great is your reward in heaven" (Luke 6:23).

Joy can begin right now—if we choose! "Rejoice in the Lord *always...!*"

SMD

The Money Game

THE PEANUT VENDOR

by Sam Kameleson

O nce upon a time, there lived a peanut vendor in South India. Every day he walked up and down the beach calling out, "Peanuts! Peanuts for sale! Peanuts!" The man was miserably poor. He barely earned half a living, hardly enough to feed his family. But at night he bragged to his wife and children, "I am the president and the vice president and the secretary and the treasurer of my own company!"

Eventually, the grinding poverty wore his nerves paper thin. One day he snapped. He sold all his peanuts and most of his meager belongings. He decided to go on a big fling.

"For one day, I am going to live like a rich man!" he vowed.

So he stopped by the barbershop for a clean shave and a hairstyle trim. He visited a fine clothing store and purchased an expensive suit, white shirt and tie, and all the accessories needed to look rich. Then he checked himself into the finest luxury hotel for the night. He had just enough money left to pay for the gourmet breakfast buffet the next morning.

He enjoyed the night's accommodations in his luxury suite. When morning came he located the private, beachfront patio for the breakfast buffet. Although it was crowded with tourists, he found a table by himself. He had just filled his plate when in walked an elegantly dressed man. By this time no more tables were available, so the man approached and asked, "May I join you?"

The peanut vendor replied, "Why, yes! Please sit down." He thought, *This is my lucky day! Not only am I living like a rich man, but I am going to eat with a rich man, too.*

As the two began to talk, the stranger asked, "Sir, what do you do?"

"I am the president and the vice president and the secretary and the treasurer of my own company," he replied. "And what do you do?"

The richly dressed man looked a bit sheepish. "I'm sorry. I should have introduced myself. I just supposed that with the coverage in the newspapers you might have recognized me. My name is John D. Rockefeller."

Although he had not recognized the face, the peanut vendor did know the name. He thought, *This is wonderful! I am eating with one of the richest men in the whole world.*

After talking for a while, Mr. Rockefeller said, "I like your style. We are starting a new company here in South India. Why don't you come to work for me? I will make you vice president of sales in my new firm."

The peanut vendor replied, "Why, thank you. What a generous offer! I would like a few minutes to think it over."

"Of course," said Mr. Rockefeller, "but I would like some indication of your interest before we part company."

The two leisurely enjoyed the rest of their meals. When they were finished, the peanut vendor stood up. He wanted to announce his decision with style. He took a step away from the table and then turned and spoke in a voice loud enough so many could overhear.

"Thank you, Mr. Rockefeller, for offering me the position of vice president in your new company. But I must decline. I prefer to be the president and the vice president and the secretary and the treasurer of my own company." He turned on his heel and walked out.

Years later, an old peanut vendor walked up and down the same resort beaches croaking in a broken voice, "Peanuts! Peanuts for sale! Peanuts!" But at night he boasted to his grandchildren that long ago one of the richest men in the world had offered to make him vice president of a huge firm.

"I turned it down," he bragged, "so I could be the president and the vice president and the secretary and the treasurer of my own company."

The peanut vendor had a chance for financial security but was too proud and self-sufficient to accept it. Yet don't we, as Christians, often make the same mistake? Our "rich" friend—our heavenly Father—owns the possessions and resources of the entire world. He has offered us love, meaning, purpose, and, ultimately, eternal life. These are His gifts to us ("And my God will meet all your needs according to his glorious riches in Jesus Christ"—Philippians 4:19). All we must do is repent of our sins and accept His lordship in our lives. But many husbands and wives are too proud—too self-sufficient—to surrender their lives and belongings to Him. The unfortunate result is that they continue in misery and poverty.

Do you struggle with wanting "more"—be it money, possessions, status, or something else? We'll spend the next few days discussing the impact of material desires and money management on marriage. As we do, keep in mind that everything we own and everything we are really belongs to the Lord of all.

JCD

WHERE IS YOUR TREASURE?

For the love of money is a root of all kinds of evil.
1 Timothy 6:10

*M*oney. Men and women have lusted for it, killed for it, died for it, and gone to hell for it. Money has come between the best of friends, fractured families, and brought down the proud and mighty. And it has torn millions of marriages limb from limb! According to Larry Burkett, founder and CEO of Christian Financial Concepts, 80 percent of couples seeking divorce say the focus of their disagreements is money.

During Jesus' time on earth, He spoke more about money than any other subject. Most of His pronouncements came in the form of warnings: "For where your treasure is, there your heart will be also" (Matthew 6:21); "What good will it be for a man if he gains the whole world, yet forfeits his soul?" (Matthew 16:26); "You cannot serve both God and Money" (Matthew 6:24).

If we want to love and serve God—and keep our marriages intact—we need to regularly examine our relationship with money, then ask: "Whom do we serve?"

Just between us...

- Have you ever had a hurtful disagreement with family or friends over money?
- How do you feel about the way we handle our finances?
- Are there ways in which we push God aside to "serve" money?
- What could we do to make sure our financial decisions are in line with Jesus' teachings?

Dear God, we confess that we're so often beguiled by the allure of money and possessions. But we want You to be Lord of our money and all our belongings. Lead us into an enduring obedience to You in this area, we pray. Amen.

THE TIN MONSTER

A man's life does not consist in the
abundance of his possessions.
Luke 12:15

t least my intentions were good. I (JCD) once ordered a swing set for my children identical to a shiny display model I'd seen at the store. What arrived, however, was a long box containing roughly 6,324 pipes, 28,487,651 bolts, 28,487,650 screws, and a set of instructions that would have befuddled Albert Einstein. For the next two days, I sweated to assemble bent parts, missing parts, and parts from a 1948 Ford thrown in just to confuse me. Finally, the wobbly construction stood upright.

I got another shock when I read the final line printed on the back of the instructions: "Please retighten all the bolts on this apparatus *every two weeks* to ensure safety and durability." I now had to devote every other Saturday to this tin monster or it would gobble up my children!

Everything you own will eventually own you! Unchecked materialism becomes your master, both when you make the purchase and when you must sweat to maintain it. That's why I heartily encourage you to decide together to own less...and *enjoy* life more.

Just between us...

- Do we have a "tin monster"—something new and supposedly valuable that's more trouble than it's worth—in our lives?
- What do we have that we don't need and could simply give or throw away?
- What guidelines could we agree on to avoid the trap of materialism?
- How can fewer possessions bring us closer to God?

Dear Lord, we are so easily driven by the desire to own more things. We want to live with less. Change us with Your truth about lasting value. We want to hold all our income and possessions in trust for You, the real owner. Amen.

HITTING THE JACKPOT

*It is easier for a camel to go through the eye of a
needle than for a rich man to enter the kingdom of God.*
Matthew 19:24

*D*o you ever dream of winning the lottery? It may interest you
to know that about a third of all lottery winners go bankrupt
within five years and that another quarter of these instant mil-
lionaires wind up selling their remaining payments at a discounted rate to
pay off debts. People who are reckless with ordinary paychecks are just as
reckless with bigger ones.

Rather than fantasize about hitting the jackpot, we should strive to
be better stewards of what we have. Handle credit cards—if you must use
them at all—with great care, and do everything you can to stay out of
debt, one of the foremost marriage destroyers. Make purchases with cash
when possible. Establish a family budget and stick to it. Remember to
give at least 10 percent of your earnings to the Lord—after all, *everything*
is His, anyway.

Above all, make sure you spend less than you earn each month. It
takes discipline, but this simple formula will go a long way toward establishing a worry-free atmosphere in your home.

Just between us...

- Most people around the world would consider the average American
  income a jackpot. Do you?
- Are we saving money instead of falling into debt?
- Would we benefit from establishing a family budget or revising the
  one we have?
- Are we tithing?

*Heavenly Father, You bless us with so much. Even when money is tight, we
know You care for us. But we often fail to be responsible and to honor You with
how we manage money. Help us to know and live by Your wisdom. Amen.*

You Can't Outgive God

See if I will not throw open the floodgates of heaven and pour out so much blessing that you will not have room enough for it.
Malachi 3:10

*M*y (JCD's) dad, an evangelist, was the original soft touch. I remember him once going off to speak in a tiny church and coming home ten days later. Eventually my mother asked about the offering. I can still see my father's face as he smiled and looked at the floor.

"You gave the money away again, didn't you?" she asked.

"Myrt," he said, "the pastor there is going through a hard time. His kids are so needy. I felt I should give the entire fifty dollars to them."

My good mother looked at my father for a few moments and then smiled. "You know, if God told you to do it, it's okay with me."

A few days later, we ran completely out of money, so my father gathered us for a time of prayer. He said, "Lord, you told us that if we would honor you in our good times, that you would take care of us when things are difficult. We need a little help at this time." The next day we received an unexpected check for $1,200. That's the way it happened—not once, but many times. No matter what you give, you'll find you can never outgive God.

Just between us...

- Are we trusting God with our giving?
- What blessings, material and nonmaterial, have we seen from our gifts?
- Do we know someone now who needs a helping hand? Should we share what we have with them?
- Do we *really* believe "God owns it all"?

Heavenly Father, You promised to pour out blessings on those who tithe in Your name. Help us to take You at Your word and to trust in Your provision as we give back to You and share our abundance with others. Amen.

EMPTY CASTLES

This very night your life will be demanded from you.
Then who will get what you have prepared for yourself?
Luke 12:20

he utter folly of materialism hit home dramatically for me (JCD) during a trip to Britain years ago. As I toured the museums and historical buildings, I was struck by what I called "empty castles." Standing there in the lonely fog were edifices constructed by proud men who thought they owned them. But where are those men today? All are gone; most are forgotten. The hollow castles they left behind stand as monuments to the vulnerability and impermanence of the men who built them.

I hope to leave more than empty castles behind when I die—something more meaningful than land, machines, stocks, or fame. I will consider my earthly existence to have been wasted unless my legacy is a loving family, a consistent investment in the lives of people, and an earnest attempt to have served the God who made me. Nothing else really matters.

Just between us...

- If we died tonight, would our obituaries describe empty pursuits or meaningful lives?
- How would the Lord judge our stewardship of money, time, and belongings?
- What has been our most foolish investment or expenditure in the past few years?
- Do we seek satisfaction in things or in the Lord? Is a change in order?
- How can we encourage each other to pursue what really matters?

Lord, we know that all that is of this earth will eventually turn to dust. How much we long to live like Your children every day—with eternity's values always in mind. Grant us Your grace and wisdom as we seek to make changes that will glorify You. Amen.

LET'S MAKE A DEAL

People who want to get rich fall into temptation and a trap.

1 Timothy 6:9

*S*ome of you are old enough to remember Monty Hall and the game show *Let's Make a Deal*—the one where contestants could keep what they had already won or risk trading it in for the mystery prize behind "door number one, door number two, or door number three." Believe it or not, I once convinced Jim to go with me to one of the shows.

There we were: I had toy birds fastened everywhere on my head and blouse, and Jim (reluctantly) held a sign that said, "My wife is for the birds." Our getup was enough to earn us seats in the contestants' row, and before we knew it, we were in front of the cameras trying to name the correct price of four items to win a brand-new Camaro. And believe me, we needed that car! Jim had just graduated from USC, and we had invested every available dollar in his tuition and expenses.

We guessed the first three items within the three-dollar margin of error, but we missed on the last one—a Hoover vacuum cleaner. So we didn't win the Camaro. Yet we walked away from that show with a new vacuum cleaner and another, much more valuable prize: a greater appreciation for how easily greed could overcome us.

Since that time we have observed that Satan appears to offer whatever a person hungers for in exchange for a spiritual compromise. In our case, a new automobile was the perfect enticement to unleash our greed. If illicit sex is your desire, it will eventually be made available. If your passion is for fame or power, the object of that lust will be promised (even if never delivered). Likewise, if you thirst for great wealth—beware! People who care passionately about money are often suckers for wild-eyed schemes and shady deals. They are always on the verge of a bonanza that seems to slip through their fingers. Instead of getting rich, they get taken.

This is the threat posed by greed. Material comforts or money in the bank can become our first love—our greatest treasure and passion. And when that happens, God becomes almost irrelevant. But the Lord will not settle for second place ("You shall have no other gods before me"— Exodus 20:3). We encourage you to say, "Let's make a deal" right now. Agree now that you'll always keep money in its place and the Lord as the first love of your life.

SMD

The Power of Encouragement

A MOST EXTRAORDINARY EVENT

by Jo Ann Larsen

Larry and Jo Ann were an ordinary couple. They lived in an ordinary house on an ordinary street. Like any other ordinary couple, they struggled to make ends meet and to do the right things for their children.

They were ordinary in yet another way—they had their squabbles. Much of their conversation concerned what was wrong in their marriage and who was to blame—until one day when a most extraordinary event took place.

"You know, Jo Ann, I've got a magic chest of drawers. Every time I open the drawers, they're full of socks and underwear," Larry said. "I want to thank you for filling them all these years."

Jo Ann stared at her husband over the top of her glasses. "What do you want, Larry?"

"Nothing. I just want you to know I appreciate those magic drawers."

This wasn't the first time Larry had done something odd, so Jo Ann pushed the incident out of her mind until a few days later.

"Jo Ann, thank you for recording so many correct check numbers in the ledger this month. You put down the right numbers fifteen out of sixteen times. That's a record."

Disbelieving what she had heard, Jo Ann looked up from her mending. "Larry, you're always complaining about my recording the wrong check numbers. Why stop now?"

"No reason. I just wanted you to know I appreciate the effort you're making."

Jo Ann shook her head and went back to her mending. "What's gotten into him?" she mumbled to herself.

Nevertheless, the next day when Jo Ann wrote a check at the grocery store, she glanced at her checkbook to confirm that she had put down the right check number. "Why do I suddenly care about those dumb check numbers?" she asked herself.

She tried to disregard the incident, but Larry's strange behavior intensified.

"Jo Ann, that was a great dinner," he said one evening. "I appreciate all your effort. Why, in the past fifteen years I'll bet you've fixed over 14,000 meals for me and the kids."

Then, "Gee, Jo Ann, the house looks spiffy. You've really worked hard to get it looking so good." And even, "Thanks, Jo Ann, for just being you. I really enjoy your company."

Jo Ann was growing worried. *Where's the sarcasm, the criticism?* she wondered.

Her fears that something peculiar was happening to her husband were confirmed by sixteen-year-old Shelly, who complained, "Dad's gone bonkers, Mom. He just told me I looked nice. Even though I'm wearing all this makeup and these sloppy clothes, he still said it. That's not Dad, Mom. What's wrong with him?"

Whatever was wrong, Larry didn't get over it. Day in and day out he continued focusing on the positive.

Over the weeks, Jo Ann grew more accustomed to her mate's unusual behavior and occasionally even gave him a grudging "Thank you." She prided herself on taking it all in stride, until one day something so peculiar happened that she became completely discombobulated.

"I want you to take a break," Larry said. "I am going to do the dishes. So please take your hands off that frying pan and leave the kitchen."

(Long, long pause.) "Thank you, Larry. Thank you very much!"

Jo Ann's step was now a little lighter, her self-confidence higher, and once in a while she hummed. She didn't seem to have as many blue moods anymore. *I rather like Larry's new behavior,* she thought.

That would be the end of the story except one day another most extraordinary event took place. This time it was Jo Ann who spoke.

"Larry," she said, "I want to thank you for going to work and providing for us all these years. I don't think I've ever told you how much I appreciate it."

No matter how hard Jo Ann has pushed for an answer, Larry has never revealed the reason for his dramatic change of behavior, and so it will likely remain one of life's mysteries. But it's one I'm thankful to live with.

You see, I am Jo Ann.

LOOKING AHEAD...

As Larry demonstrated, a little encouragement can transform a marriage. None of us—king or queen, president or business leader, husband, housewife or child—is without the human craving for appreciation. Mark Twain once said, "I can live for two months on a good compliment." A kind word is like that. It fuels our energy and infuses us with new enthusiasm for facing the challenges life throws our way.

I invite you during this week's discussion to consider the incredible power of encouragement. As you apply each principle, I think you'll find that the sun shines a little brighter and your day runs a bit smoother. You might begin by simply telling your partner how much you appreciate having him or her around.

JCD

SIDE BY SIDE

Encourage one another daily.
Hebrews 3:13

*T*he Greek translation for the word *encouragement* is *parakletos*, which literally means "called alongside to help." It brings to mind the scriptural image of two people yoked side by side, as when Jesus said, "Take my yoke upon you and learn from me.... For my yoke is easy and my burden is light" (Matthew 11:29–30). This kind of encouragement includes offering an uplifting word, but it is more than that. It is standing by your husband and keeping an attitude of good cheer when he is laid off his job. It is pitching in to finish the dishes when your wife is too tired to stand. It's crouching down to a four-year-old's eye level and listening sympathetically as she tearfully tells you about her skinned knee.

The act of encouraging *doesn't* include instructing your partner on what to do about a problem. It doesn't include giving advice, offering tips for improving in the future, or uttering hollow words such as "You really should have known better than to make that foolish mistake" or "Get over it." Instead, encouragement is a participation game. When you stand alongside your mate and share his or her troubles, you've become a practitioner of *parakletos* and an exceptional source of courage, hope, and happiness.

Just between us...

- Do you know anyone who always makes you feel good about yourself? How do they do it?
- Why is it often so difficult to think about the other person first?
- How has God used me to "come alongside" you? How can I do better?

Lord Jesus, thank You that You put it within our power to encourage others. May we grow in that ministry. May we become experts at it—starting in our marriage. Amen.

TRANSFORMING LOVE

In all our distress and persecution we were encouraged....
1 Thessalonians 3:7

When I (JCD) was thirteen, we adopted the most wonderful dog in the world. Penny, as we called him, was smart and obedient. He loved everybody, and everybody loved him. But when I went off to college and my parents moved, our family reluctantly decided to give Penny away to another family.

After a while, Penny decided that my father wasn't coming back. The dog began to grieve. In fact, he seemed to give up on life, and before long, arthritis and other problems left him paralyzed. When my father heard about Penny's sad state, he drove seven hundred miles to bring him home. He found our dog curled up in a little ball, unable to move. But Penny's tiny stub of a tail thrashed wildly when he saw his master. Remarkably, with the love and attention my parents began to shower on him, Penny recovered. Within two weeks of returning home, he was running and jumping. He lived eleven more years without another sign of arthritis!

This story about our family dog reminds me that if even a mutt needs love and encouragement to stay alive, then so does every human being on the face of the earth. We are social beings, designed to depend on God and each other. Yet some of us are curled up in a pitiful little ball of discouragement.

Every day we have the power to bring life by giving encouragement to others—or we can ignore their needs and think only of ourselves. The choice is ours.

Just between us...

- Has my encouragement ever made you feel transformed or "healed"?
- Who might be transformed by a little encouragement from us?

Lord, open our eyes to others' need for attention, affection, and encouragement. May we never withhold what is our duty and privilege to give. Amen.

STICKS AND STONES

The poison of vipers is on their lips.
Psalm 140:3

*T*he old adage "sticks and stones may break my bones, but words will never hurt me" simply isn't true. Anyone who has felt the stinging barb of criticism knows that words can deeply wound. Lewis Yablonsky, author of *Fathers and Sons,* observed the effect such negative comments had on his own father. At the dinner table, Lewis's mother would say things like, "Look at your father! His shoulders are bent down; he's a failure. He doesn't have the courage to get a better job or make more money. He's a beaten man." Yablonsky's father never defended himself. He just kept staring at his plate.

Psychologist and author Abraham Maslow once said, "It takes nine affirming comments to make up for each critical comment we give to our children." Adults aren't immune to criticism and put-downs either. Let's focus on the positive traits our partner brings to our marriage. Why not list them? Then point them out—daily and lovingly—to our mate.

Just between us...

- Is there a negative comment from your childhood that stays with you? How did it make you feel?
- Do we need to be more affirming and less critical? How can we improve?
- How did Jesus affirm others? (For examples, look at Matthew 16:17–19; 26:6–13; Luke 7:44–48; and John 1:47–48.)
- In what areas of your life are you discouraged? How can I lift you up?

Dear Father, we're deeply sorry for any harmful words we've aimed at each other lately. Please forgive us, and help us to forgive each other. We long to do better at using only words that build, heal, encourage, and affirm. Help us, we pray. Amen.

ERROR OR OPPORTUNITY?

An anxious heart weighs a man down,
but a kind word cheers him up.
Proverbs 12:25

*M*any years ago, at what was then Standard Oil Company, an executive's mistake cost the firm more than two million dollars. On the day the news leaked, the firm's employees feared the wrath of the powerful head of the company—John D. Rockefeller—and found various ways to avoid him. One partner, however, kept his previously scheduled appointment. When he walked into the president's office, he saw Rockefeller writing on a pad of paper.

"Oh, it's you, Bedford," Rockefeller said calmly. "I suppose you've heard about our loss?" The partner said that he had. "I've been thinking it over," Rockefeller said, "and before I ask the man to discuss the matter, I've been making some notes." Across the top of the page was written, "Points in favor of Mr. _____." There followed a long list of the man's virtues, including a description of how the executive had helped the firm make the right decision on three separate occasions. Since the earnings from these decisions had added up to many times the cost of the recent error, Rockefeller told Bedford that he had decided to seize the opportunity to encourage the executive instead of censure him.

The next time your spouse fails you, you could cut him or her down in a torrent of angry words...or you could see a golden opportunity to encourage.

Just between us...

- When was I most encouraging to you during a crisis?
- Is there a particular Scripture verse you cling to during tough times?

Lord, we so often underestimate how much influence our words can have. We ask for wisdom to speak encouragement—especially when criticism might be expected. Amen.

Your Father's Arms

May our Lord Jesus Christ himself and God our Father...
encourage your hearts and strengthen you.
2 Thessalonians 2:16–17

A talented young athlete, the son of a star baseball player, was struggling in the minor leagues and expected to be released any day. During one game, he came to bat having already struck out once and quickly rang up two more strikes. Then the catcher trotted away for a conference with the pitcher. The umpire, standing behind the plate, spoke to the young man. "You hold the bat just the way your dad held it," he said. "I can see his genes in you. You have your father's arms." On the next pitch, the young man knocked the ball out of the park. His play improved remarkably, and soon he was called up to the major leagues. When asked what changed his game, the young man gave credit to the umpire's words. "After that," he explained, "whenever I swung the bat, I just imagined that I was using Dad's arms instead of my own."

In your ministry of encouragement in your marriage, remember to use your Father's arms. Maybe you recall the biblical example of Barnabas, whose name means "son of encouragement." The Bible says he was "full of the Holy Spirit and faith" (Acts 11:24), and his gift was invaluable in helping the apostle Paul lead others to Christ during their missionary journeys.

Do you sometimes feel inadequate to help others? God Himself is ready to encourage you—and to bless you with His strength to encourage those you love.

Just between us...

- What's your favorite form of encouragement?
- In what ways do I encourage you without words?
- How can we best tap into God's resources to encourage each other?

Almighty God, thank You for Your gifts of encouragement and comfort to us. Help us to draw on Your strength as we encourage one another. Amen.

BEHIND EVERY SUCCESS...

Let us encourage one another.
Hebrews 10:25

*I*t's been said that behind every successful man is a great woman. The wife of one of the most famous names in literature, Nathaniel Hawthorne, was probably one such woman. Sophia Hawthorne secretly set aside a few dollars each week, a savings that eventually grew large enough to support them both for a year. You see, Sophia believed that her husband would one day be a great writer. When Hawthorne came home and announced in disgrace that he'd been fired from his job in a customhouse, Sophia presented him with the money, saying, "Now you can write your book!" Her confidence and encouragement led to one of America's classic novels, *The Scarlet Letter.*

Then there was the corporate chief who, while traveling with his wife, pulled their car into a rundown gas station. They discovered that his wife had dated the gas station attendant in high school. "Boy, are you lucky I came along," bragged the husband after they left. "If you had married him, you would be the wife of a gas station attendant."

"My dear," replied the wife, "if I had married him, he would be the chief executive officer, and you would be the gas station attendant."

It's certainly true that one spouse has tremendous influence on the success of the other. Jim has supported me in my spiritual life, in the raising of our children, and in so many other areas. Likewise, I have attempted to bolster him however I could and have seen God's blessing on his work and ministry. And Jim lets me know he appreciates my encouragement. He has said more than once that I believed in him before he believed in himself. Of course, we've fallen short of this supportive ideal on more than one occasion—and you probably will, too. But if you consistently strive to bring strong and steady encouragement to your mate, you'll both reap lasting rewards.

SMD

To Fight or
Not to Fight?

THE ARGUMENT

by Gigi Graham Tchividjian

e walked out, closing the door firmly behind him. I heard the car drive away, and with a heavy, aching heart, I leaned against the closed door. Hot, angry tears filled my eyes, spilled over, and ran down my cheeks.

How had it happened? How had things built to this point? Neither of us had intended our little discussion to develop into a heated disagreement. But it was late, and we had both experienced a hard day.

Stephan had risen early to drive for the car pool. Then he had seen several patients with difficult, heartbreaking problems. An emergency had taken up his lunch break, and he had been behind schedule for the rest of the afternoon. When he finally left the office, he hit a traffic jam on the freeway and arrived home tense and tired to a wife with seven children, all demanding his attention.

I, too, had endured a difficult day after a sleepless night with the baby. Besides the normal responsibilities involved with running a home, rain had kept us confined indoors all day. It was humid, and the children were more quarrelsome than usual, amusing themselves by picking on each other. Between settling arguments and soothing hurt feelings, I managed to get dinner on the table. But I hadn't had time to comb my hair or freshen my makeup, and Stephan could sense my frustration when he came in.

Finally, when the kitchen was clean, the small children bathed and tucked into bed, and the teenagers talked out, Stephan and I found ourselves alone in our bedroom, trying to discuss a minor problem. It soon blew out of proportion. Angry feelings were vented, words spoken that we did not mean, and then—a slammed door and retreating car.

I slumped into a chair, dissolving into tears of discouragement and disappointment in myself. How long was it going to take to learn my lesson? Late at night, especially after a wearisome day, is not the time for arguing, but for comfort, encouragement, and loving. As I sat there, I remembered that I had been so busy trying to handle the home front, keeping everything and everyone under control, that I had not spent time with the Lord that day. I had even failed to pray for Stephan. No wonder things had not gone well.

I glanced in the mirror and saw red, puffy eyes, no makeup, and hair in disarray. I saw lines of fatigue and tension where there should have been tenderness and love, and I understood Stephan's desire to get away and cool off.

I fell on my knees beside the chair, asking the Lord to forgive me and to fill me with His Holy Spirit so I could be to Stephan all he had ever dreamed. I asked for the Lord's strength, His sensitivity, His wisdom, so I could juggle my own schedule, the demands of my home and children, and still have time to meet my husband's needs when he came home from the day's work. Then I added a timid P. S. asking Him to give Stephan a change of heart, too.

I felt peace and a sudden refreshing. I got up, washed my face, added a little color to my cheeks and lips, combed my hair, lavished perfume on myself, and climbed into bed to wait.

Before long, I heard the front door open and familiar footsteps in the brick hallway. Our bedroom door opened quietly and Stephan stood there, his tired face and kind, loving eyes drawing me like a magnet. I flew into his arms. Later, our loving erased the last traces of frustration and anger. Clinging to each other as we fell into a much-needed sleep, I couldn't help wondering why we hadn't thought of this in the first place.

Conflict in marriage is inevitable: You can't live with someone every day of your life without occasional friction. In too many of today's marriages, however, fights are the rule rather than the exception.

A sixth-grade teacher shared with me the results of a writing project assigned to her class. She asked the kids to complete a series of sentences that began with the phrase "I wish...." She was shocked and saddened by the response. Instead of writing about toys, animals, and trips to theme parks, twenty of the thirty kids made reference to the breakup of their families or conflict at home.

Let's talk this next week about what we can do to reduce conflict in marriage and to make sure that when we do disagree, it's something worth arguing about.

JCD

DIFFERING ASSUMPTIONS

May the God who gives endurance and encouragement give you
a spirit of unity among yourselves as you follow Christ Jesus.
Romans 15:5

s in last night's story, "The Argument," a difficult day can quickly lead to an unnecessarily heated exchange between spouses. Fatigue, problems with the kids or job, illness, or financial worries can make anyone more susceptible to a fight. So can the condition I (JCD) call "differing assumptions."

For example, after a particularly grueling series of speaking appearances some years ago, I came dragging home on Friday night feeling I'd earned a day off. I planned to watch a USC-Alabama football game on TV the next day. That seemed like a reasonable plan for a guy who had been out earning a living day and night. Shirley, on the other hand, had been running our home and watching the kids for six weeks and felt it was time I pitched in on a few chores. It was entirely reasonable for Shirley to think that she deserved some help at home after doing "domestic duty" for six weeks. Our assumptions collided about ten o'clock Saturday morning. Harsh words froze our relationship for three days. It was a stupid fight, but understandable in light of factors like overwork, fatigue, selfishness, and very different views of what the other was thinking.

When we're making our own plans we need to remember to consider our partner's mental and physical state. During stressful circumstances, we should take extra care to communicate our expectations ahead of time.

Just between us...

- Have differing assumptions caused us to argue recently?
- How can I do a better job of being aware of your mood?
- Do we communicate our expectations ahead of time?

Lord, by Your Spirit, help us to be aware of each other's needs and to take care in our communication. Draw us together in unity and in love of You. Amen.

FIGHT FAIR

Remind the people...to be peaceable and considerate,
and to show true humility toward all.

Titus 3:1–2

*S*ince some conflict in marriage is inevitable, learning to fight
fair just might be the most important skill a couple can master. The key is to understand the difference between healthy
and unhealthy combat.

In an unstable marriage, hostility is aimed at the partner's soft under-
belly with comments such as "You never do anything right!" "Why did I
marry you in the first place?" and "You're getting more like your mother
every day!" These offensive remarks strike at the heart of self-worth.
Healthy conflict, by contrast, focuses on the issues that cause disagreement: "It upsets me when you don't tell me you're going to be late for
dinner," or "I was embarrassed when you made me look foolish at the
party last night." Can you hear the difference?

Even though these approaches may be equally contentious, the first
assaults the dignity of the partner, while the second addresses the source
of conflict. Couples who learn this important distinction are much better prepared to work through disagreements without wounds and insults.

Just between us...

* When we have a fight, are we more likely to attack the person and
  miss the problem, or to attack the problem and protect the person?
* What did Jesus say about yielding to others when we are unfairly
  attacked or criticized? (See Matthew 5:38–41; Luke 6:27–31.)
* How would doing a better job of fighting fair help our relationship?
* How can we support each other in doing this?

Father, we need Your help to show love and respect while we resolve differences.
We don't want disagreements to hurt the relationship You've graciously given
us. We know Your power and wisdom can be ours each day, and we humbly
ask for them. Amen.

THE LINE OF RESPECT

Show proper respect to everyone.
1 Peter 2:17

onflict can often play a positive role in marriage—especially when it helps maintain lines of respect.

Suppose I (JCD) work at my office two hours later than usual on a particular night. I know that Shirley is preparing a candlelight dinner, yet I don't call to let her know I'll be late. As the evening wears on, Shirley wraps the cold food in foil and puts it in the refrigerator. When I finally get home, I don't apologize. Instead, I sit down with the newspaper and abruptly tell Shirley to get my dinner ready. You can bet there would be fireworks in the Dobson household that night! Shirley would rightfully interpret my insensitive behavior as insulting and would move to defend the "line of respect" between us. Her strong feelings would be totally justified.

Let's put the shoe on the other foot. Suppose Shirley knows I need the car at 2:00 P.M. for some important purpose, but she deliberately keeps me waiting. Perhaps she sits in a restaurant with a friend, drinking coffee and talking. Meanwhile, I'm pacing the floor at home wondering where she is. It is very likely that she will hear about my dissatisfaction when she gets home. Even though the offense was minor, the line of respect has been violated.

Some things are worth defending. At the top of the list is the "line of respect" between husbands and wives.

Just between us...

- When was the last time we had a fight that was good for our relationship?
- Have I crossed your line of respect recently?
- How will upholding the line of respect improve our marriage?

Dear Lord, we want to show respect for each other, but we confess that we're too often self-centered and insensitive. Forgive us, Lord. Grant us Your grace as we defend the mutual rights that are the foundation of our affection. Amen.

AFTER THE FIGHT

Do not let the sun go down while you are still angry.
Ephesians 4:26

*S*ometimes it's not the fight itself that's damaging, but what happens when the battle is over. Think for a moment about your own verbal spats with your mate. Do they usually result in a time of healing, or are issues left hanging for a "rematch" later on? Do you and your spouse agree to leave an argument behind after you've talked it out, or is there a prolonged period of distance and silence?

In unstable marriages, conflict is never entirely resolved. Resentment and hurt feelings accumulate over time and eventually turn to bile in the soul, which then erodes the relationship from within. But in healthy relationships, confrontation allows ventilation that ends in forgiveness, a drawing together, and a better understanding of each other.

After an argument with your spouse, ask yourself these four important questions: *Are there things I've said or done that have grieved my partner? Do I need to ask forgiveness for attacking the self-worth of my spouse? Have I refused to let go of an issue even though I said it was settled? Are there substantive matters that haven't been resolved?* Then move to put an end to the conflict—before the sun goes down.

Just between us...

- In our last fight, did we resolve the issue in question?
- Do our conflicts usually end positively, or with hurt feelings and unanswered questions?
- What changes would help us resolve conflicts "before the sun goes down"?

Lord, give us the maturity and strength to settle our disagreements quickly and without damaging the personhood of each other. We know that this is Your will for us, but we need Your guidance to live by it. Amen.

HOLY MOTIVES

*If you obey my commands, you will remain in my love, just as
I have obeyed my Father's commands and remain in his love.*

John 15:10

During Jesus' time on earth, He was the epitome of love and compassion—yet He was also surrounded by conflict. He didn't hesitate to set the Pharisees straight when they spoke or acted against God's will. Jesus even rebuked Peter when His disciple rejected the prophecy that Christ would suffer and die (Mark 8:31–33). But Jesus' motives were pure and perfect. He never intended His words to harm His listeners; rather, He spoke from a heart of love for His children.

We urge you to consider your motives when the temptation arises to do battle with your mate. Is your aim to lovingly enlighten, or to prove you are "right"? Are you reacting to another problem that has nothing to do with your partner? Is this really an important issue, or are you just blowing off steam at the expense of your spouse?

As long as we remember Christ's motives for conflict and follow His example, we will "remain in his love," and our marriages will move down the right path.

Just between us...

- During our last dispute, did you feel that my goal was to "lovingly enlighten," or to win the battle?
- During conflicts in our marriage, how can we be more like Jesus?
- Have I wounded your spirit during times of disagreement? If so, will you forgive me?

Lord Jesus, You were no stranger to the challenges of conflict, and we thank You for Your inspiring example. How much we want to be like You and to do Your will. Show us Your wisdom in new ways as we seek to mature in this area. Amen.

WHEN THE TOP FLIES OFF

Be of one mind, live in peace.
And the God of love and peace will be with you.
2 Corinthians 13:11

*B*ecause of our family ministry and Jim's background as a psychologist, I sometimes wonder if people think that our marriage is somehow "different"—that we live in a dreamlike state of wedded bliss where conflict doesn't exist. Believe me, that's just not the case. We do our share of fussing and face the same struggles you do, whether it's motivated by fatigue, worry about the kids, not communicating our expectations properly, or something else.

I recall an incident after we were engaged that seems funny now, but wasn't so amusing at the time. Jim owned a 1949 Mercury convertible called "Old Red." It was a disaster. The top wouldn't go up or down; the electric windows didn't work; the lights sometimes went out unexpectedly; and the engine had a habit of dying regularly. Every Sunday afternoon we took it out for a push. Worse, the front seat had springs sticking out at odd angles that snagged my clothes and made for a most uncomfortable ride. I hated that car, but Jim didn't want to go into debt to buy a new one.

The coup de grace came the day Jim picked me up for an important job interview. I was wearing my best outfit, a black suit. As we sped down the road at fifty miles per hour, the convertible top suddenly blew off. Bits of string and canvas beat at our heads as dust flew everywhere. The remnants of the old top hooked onto the back of the car and flapped in the air like Superman's cape.

Jim was so irritated at the car that he wouldn't stop. He just kept barreling down the highway with the ribs of the top glistening above us. I screamed at him from under the dashboard, where I was crouched to escape the pieces of Old Red that were still flying about. Between his car falling apart and my screaming, Jim got even angrier.

Somehow we survived the day when both of us—and Old Red—blew our tops. Jim bought a newer car a few months later and, more importantly, we didn't call off our engagement!

That's how life is when you climb into the marvelous vehicle called marriage. You're in for a long and wonderful ride. Expect the unexpected to happen. It will probably rattle your nerves and set you at odds with each other, and the top may even blow off every now and then. But if you share a committed love, you *can* survive those unexpected and unwanted conflicts. We have—for forty years now.

SMD

Will You Forgive Me?

"THE FACE OF MY ENEMY"

by Corrie ten Boom

*I*t was in a church in Munich that I saw him—a balding, heavyset man in a gray overcoat, a brown felt hat clutched between his hands. People were filing out of the basement room where I had just spoken and moving along the rows of wooden chairs to the door at the rear. The year was 1947, and I had come from Holland to defeated Germany with the message that God forgives.

This was the truth they needed most to hear in that bitter, bombed-out land, and I gave them my favorite mental picture. Maybe because the sea is never far from a Hollander's mind, I liked to think that that's where forgiven sins were thrown. "When we confess our sins," I said, "God casts them into the deepest ocean, gone forever. And even though I cannot find a Scripture for it, I believe God then places a sign out there that says, 'NO FISHING ALLOWED.'"

The solemn faces stared back at me, not quite daring to believe. There were never questions after a talk in Germany in 1947. People stood up in silence, collected their wraps in silence, left the room in silence.

And that's when I saw him working his way forward against the others. One moment I saw the overcoat and the brown hat; the next, a blue uniform and a visored cap with its skull and crossbones. It came back with a rush: the huge room with its harsh overhead lights, the pathetic pile of dresses and shoes in the center of the floor, the shame of walking naked past this man. I could see my sister's frail form ahead of me, ribs sharp beneath the parchment skin. *Betsie, how thin you were!*

The place was Ravensbruck, and the man who was making his way forward had been a guard—one of the cruelest guards.

Now he was in front of me, hand thrust out: "A fine message, Fräulein! How good it is to know that, as you say, all our sins are at the bottom of the sea!"

And I, who had spoken so glibly of forgiveness, fumbled in my pocketbook rather than take that hand. He would not remember me, of course—how could he remember one prisoner among those thousands of women?

But I remembered him and the leather crop swinging from his belt. I was face-to-face with one of my captors, and my blood seemed to freeze.

"You mentioned Ravensbruck in your talk," he was saying. "I was a guard there." No, he did not remember me.

"But since that time," he went on, "I have become a Christian. I know that God has forgiven me for the cruel things I did there, but I would like to hear it from your lips as well. Fräulein"—again the hand came out—"will you forgive me?"

And I stood there—I whose sins had again and again needed to be forgiven—and could not forgive. Betsie had died in that place—could he erase her slow, terrible death simply by the asking?

It could not have been many seconds that he stood there—hand held out—but to me it seemed hours as I wrestled with the most difficult thing I had ever had to do.

For I had to do it—I knew that. The message that God forgives has a prior condition: that we forgive those who have injured us. "If you do not forgive men their trespasses," Jesus says, "neither will your Father in Heaven forgive your trespasses."

I knew it not only as a commandment of God, but as a daily experience. Since the end of the war I had had a home in Holland for victims of Nazi brutality. Those who were able to forgive their former enemies were also able to return to the outside world and rebuild their lives, no matter what the physical scars. Those who nursed their bitterness remained invalids. It was as simple and horrible as that.

And still I stood there with the coldness clutching my heart. But forgiveness is not an emotion—I knew that, too. Forgiveness is an act of the will, and the will can function regardless of the temperature of the heart. *Jesus, help me!* I prayed silently. *I can lift my hand. I can do that much. You supply the feeling.*

So, woodenly and mechanically, I thrust my hand into the one stretched out to me. And as I did, an incredible thing took place. The current started in my shoulder, raced down my arm, and sprang into our joined hands. And then this healing warmth seemed to flood my whole being, bringing tears to my eyes.

"I forgive you, brother!" I cried. "With all my heart."

For a long moment, we grasped each other's hands—the former guard and the former prisoner. I had never known God's love so intensely as I did then. But even so, I realized it was not my love. I had tried and did not have the power. It was the power of the Holy Spirit as recorded in Romans 5:5: "Because God has poured out his love into our hearts by the Holy Spirit, whom he has given us."

LOOKING AHEAD...

I can't imagine any situation or circumstance in which the obligation to forgive would be more difficult than the one Corrie faced. She had lived with routine murder, humiliation, cruelty, and starvation at the hands of the man who now faced her. Every natural impulse—every angry emotion—would cry out for revenge against her former tormentor. She still carried with her the images of her father, emaciated sister, and other family members who died at the hands of the Nazis. I wonder if I could have had the moral strength to forgive this guard and release the passion for revenge and retribution. Yet, Corrie ten Boom was able to do just that and thereby show the world what Jesus meant by His commandment to "turn the other cheek."

Here's the question of the hour: If Corrie ten Boom could forgive her captors—and if Jesus could forgive the Roman soldiers and you and me for killing Him on the cross—can't we find it in our hearts to forgive the mistakes and hurtful actions of our imperfect mate? We absolutely must, or we'll become pathetic invalids trapped by bitterness and hate.

JCD

FINDING THE STRENGTH TO FORGIVE

*"If you hold anything against anyone, forgive him, so
that your Father in heaven may forgive you your sins."*
Mark 11:25

orgiveness is never easy, but it's the vital first step toward
healing. A woman once wrote to tell "Dear Abby" that her
husband of two years had had an affair with a young widow,
who then carried his child. The wife wanted to die; she also wanted to kill
her husband and the widow. But she knew those weren't the answers she
needed. Instead she prayed to God, and the Lord gave her the strength to
forgive both the husband and the widow.

The baby was born in the home of the husband and wife and raised
as their own. He turned out to be their only child. In fifty years, wife and
husband never discussed the incident again. "But," the wife wrote, "I've
read the love and gratitude in his eyes a thousand times."

By praying for God's help, this woman received peace, a loving marriage, and a child she otherwise wouldn't have had. The next time anger
and resentment rise up in your throat, get on your knees and ask the Lord
for the healing work He wants to do in your heart. We believe He will
hear and answer that prayer.

Just between us...

- Who in your life has been most difficult to forgive? Why?
- Is there someone you have never forgiven?
- How has God honored the times you've forgiven someone?
- Do we have anything that calls for forgiveness between us? What?
- How will forgiving now make our marriage stronger in the future?

*Dear Lord Jesus, forgiveness sometimes costs so much and hurts even more! But
You forgave us—and now You ask us to forgive others. Teach us the healing
power of forgiveness. Help us to bring this gift of love to our marriage again
and again. Amen.*

THE COST OF BITTERNESS

"I tell you, [forgive] not seven times,
but seventy-seven times."
Matthew 18:22

*J*ust as we must act on Scripture's instruction to forgive, we should also consider the great cost of failing to do so. Withholding forgiveness brings on bitterness, which Neal T. Anderson says is like "battery acid in the soul." It leads to anger, resentment, depression, health problems, isolation, struggles with addictions, and more. It continues to haunt the person until he or she comes to terms with it. People who hang on to bitterness cause more pain to themselves than to the targets of their wrath.

A second cost is equally distressing. Jesus told a parable of an unmerciful servant who, after his master forgave him a large debt, demanded payment of a small debt from another servant. The master had the first servant thrown into jail and tortured. "This is how my heavenly Father will treat each of you," Jesus said, "unless you forgive your brother from your heart" (Matthew 18:35).

For couples who want to follow God's way for marriage and who hope for His best in their relationship, forgiveness is not just a suggestion. It is a spiritual commandment!

Just between us...

• Why is failing to forgive more damaging to us than to the one who wronged us?
• Are either of us bitter about something today? Why?
• What steps of forgiveness can we take together?
• How can we avoid bitterness in the future?

Dear Lord, You have spoken plainly about the consequences of withholding forgiveness. Help us to hear You and obey. May we please You and bless each other with our quickness to forgive at all times. Amen.

"I CHOOSE TO FORGIVE"

Forgive as the Lord forgave you.
Colossians 3:13

C S. Lewis pointed out that "forgiving does not mean excusing...if that were so, there would be nothing to forgive." The people of Paducah, Kentucky, understood this. A few years ago, fourteen-year-old Michael Carneal opened fire on a group of students who had gathered in prayer. In seconds, ten were wounded, three fatally. Yet the students and people from the community showed a remarkable willingness to forgive. Placards appeared at the high school reading, "We Forgive You, Mike." Kelly Carneal, Michael's sister, was not only embraced by her peers, but was also asked to sing in the choir at the slain girls' funeral. During the town's annual Christmas parade, the people lifted up a moment of silent prayer on behalf of Michael and his family. One young girl said it best: "I can hate Michael and bear the scars of what he did for the rest of my life. But I choose to forgive him and get beyond it."

Dr. Arch Hart, a Christian psychologist says, "Forgiveness is giving up my right to hurt you for hurting me." Forgiving is a decision, not an emotion. In our marriages we'll often need to choose to have a right attitude before our wounded heart has healed. Even when we can't control how we feel, we can determine how we act and what we do with our pain.

Just between us...

- How did Jesus model forgiveness for us?
- Is there someone in our family, our community, or our circle of acquaintances who has committed a widely known injustice? How can we show this person forgiveness?
- Is it necessary to forget in order to forgive?

Lord, thank You for showing us how to forgive. May we choose to forgive in our marriage—even when we don't feel like it. We trust You to bring healing in our feelings and memories in Your time. Amen.

ADMIT YOU'RE WRONG

If we confess our sins, he is faithful
and just and will forgive us our sins.
1 John 1:9

It is very difficult for parents to ask their children for forgiveness. They feel that it somehow damages their authority to admit they have done wrong and promise to do better next time. But I (JCD) believe it is healthy for a mom and dad to model for a child how to apologize when they have done something wrong.

One evening years ago, I was especially grouchy with my ten-year-old daughter, Danae. I blamed her for things that weren't her fault and upset her needlessly. After I went to bed, I realized that I needed to apologize. The next morning I said, "Danae, I'm sure you know that daddies are not perfect human beings. I know I wasn't fair with you last night. I was terribly grouchy, and I'm asking you to forgive me." Danae put her arms around me, then shocked me to my toes when she said, "I knew you were going to have to apologize, Daddy, and it's okay. I forgive you!"

If parents never admit their wrongs, their children often remember the offenses well into adulthood. Instead of clearing the air and reestablishing the relationship, the hurt feelings are stored in the memory bank to fester. Furthermore, by admitting a wrong, the parent says on the record that things will change—that he or she will try not to make the same mistake in the future. Healthy families follow these principles of forgiveness...from the top down!

Just between us...

- Why is it easy to overlook the need to ask our children for pardon?
- When we ask for forgiveness from our kids, what do we demonstrate?

Heavenly Father, it's never easy to admit we're wrong—especially to children. Give us the courage to seek forgiveness from our kids whenever it's warranted. May our family grow up without lingering bitterness and hurt. Amen.

THE PRIDE ROADBLOCK

I hate pride and arrogance.
Proverbs 8:13

*I*n the middle of your highway to forgiveness there may be a giant roadblock called *pride*. You know in your heart that you offended your wife with that comment about her body, or her intelligence, or her family. You realize you hurt your husband with that remark about his selfishness or his waste of money. But something is keeping you from admitting wrong and seeking forgiveness. Even though you know you're guilty, you can't get the words out of your mouth. At best you can mumble, "I'm sorry," but you don't really want to know if your partner heard you.

Pride is terribly destructive to human relationships. It may be the sin that God hates most, because there are more than one hundred references to it in Scripture. Proverbs 6:17–19 describes seven things that God finds detestable, and the first one on the list is "a proud look." If you or your mate have a haughty attitude that prevents you from seeking forgiveness and reconciling, it *will* damage your marriage. We encourge you to swallow your pride and talk to your spouse. Once you've done that, why not clear one more roadblock and seek the Lord's forgiveness for your prideful heart?

Just between us...

- Has my pride kept us apart in the past? How?
- In what ways has swallowing our pride blessed us in the past?
- How can we break down the roadblock of pride on our way to a stronger relationship?

Dear Lord Jesus, thank You for Your example of humility and mercy. Forgive us for our stubborn, prideful treatment of each other. We want to change. Help us to lay aside pride, admit wrongs, and humbly ask for forgiveness. Amen.

BLACK SUNDAY

*"If he sins against you seven times in a day, and seven
times comes back to you and says, 'I repent,' forgive him."*
Luke 17:4

Every family has moments they'd rather forget—moments that later call for understanding and forgiveness. When our children lived at home, we found that Sunday was often the most frustrating day of the week, especially during the "get 'em ready for church" routine. But Black Sunday was uniquely chaotic!

Jim and I began the day by getting up late, which meant that everyone had to rush to prepare for church. Then there was the matter of spilled milk at breakfast and the black shoe polish on the floor. Finally, Ryan, who was dressed first, managed to slip out the back door and get himself dirty from head to toe. As these irritations mounted, the criticism and accusations flew back and forth. At least one spanking was delivered and another three or four were promised.

After the Sunday evening service we called the family together. We described the day we'd had and asked each person to forgive us for our part in it. We also gave each member of the family a chance to express his or her feelings. Ryan was given his first shot, and he fired it at me. "You've been a real grouch today, Mom!" he said with feeling. "You've blamed me for everything all day long." Danae then poured out her hostilities and frustrations. Finally, Jim and I had an opportunity to explain the tensions that had caused our overreaction. It was a valuable time of ventilation and honesty that drew us together once more. We then had prayer as a family and asked the Lord to help us live and work together in love and harmony.

No matter how hard we try, we will experience times when we fail to live up to our Christian principles. When those times arrive, discussion and forgiveness are the best methods for soothing wounded relationships. I urge you at those moments to actively seek forgiveness from each other and from God and freely offer forgiveness in return.

While you're at it, forgive yourself. If God can post a "No Fishing" sign by the sea where your sins are thrown, then so can you and I.

SMD

You Are a Treasure

JOHNNY LINGO'S EIGHT-COW WIFE

by Patricia McGerr

When I visited the South Pacific islands, I took a notebook along. I had a three-week leave between assignments in Japan, so I borrowed a boat and sailed to Kiniwata. The notebook was supposed to help me become a junior-grade Maugham or Michener. But when I got back, among all my notes the only sentence that still interested me was the one that said, "Johnny Lingo gave eight cows to Sarita's father."

Johnny Lingo wasn't exactly his name. But I wrote it down that way because I learned about the eight cows from Shenkin, the fat manager of the guest house at Kiniwata. He was from Chicago and had a habit of Americanizing the names of the islanders. He wasn't the only one who talked about Johnny, though. His name came up with many people in many connections. If I wanted to spend a few days on the island of Nurabandi, a day's sail away, Johnny Lingo could put me up, they told me, since he had built a five-room house—unheard-of luxury! If I wanted to fish, he could show me where the biting was best. If I wanted fresh vegetables, his garden was the greenest. If I sought pearls, his business savvy would bring me the best buys. Oh, the people of Kiniwata all spoke highly of Johnny Lingo. Yet when they spoke, they smiled, and the smiles were slightly mocking.

"Get Johnny Lingo to help you find what you want, and then let him do the bargaining," advised Shenkin, as I sat on the veranda of his guest house wondering whether to visit Nurabandi. "He'll earn his commission four times over. Johnny knows values and how to make a deal."

"Johnny Lingo!" The chubby boy on the veranda steps hooted the name, then hugged his knees and rocked with shrill laughter.

"What goes on?" I asked. "Everybody around here tells me to get in touch with Johnny Lingo and then breaks up. Let me in on the joke."

"They like to laugh," Shenkin said. He shrugged his heavy shoulders.

"And Johnny's the brightest, the quickest, the strongest young man in all this group of islands. So they like best to laugh at him."

"But if he's all you say, what is there to laugh about?"

"Only one thing. Five months ago, at fall festival time, Johnny came to Kiniwata and found himself a wife. He paid her father eight cows!"

He spoke the last words with great solemnity. I knew enough about island customs to be thoroughly impressed. Two or three cows would buy a fair-to-middling wife; four or five a highly satisfactory one.

"Eight cows!" I said. "She must be a beauty who takes your breath away."

"The kindest could only call Sarita plain," was Shenkin's answer. "She was skinny. She walked with her shoulders hunched and her head ducked. She was scared of her own shadow."

"Then how do you explain the eight cows?"

"We don't," he said. "And that's why the villagers grin when they talk about Johnny. They get special satisfaction from the fact that Johnny, the sharpest trader in the islands, was bested by Sarita's father, dull old Sam Karoo."

"Eight cows," I said unbelievingly. "I'd like to meet this Johnny Lingo."

So the next afternoon I sailed a boat to Nurabandi and met Johnny at his home, where I asked about his eight-cow purchase of Sarita. I assumed he had done it for his own vanity and reputation—at least until Sarita walked into the room. She was the most beautiful woman I have ever seen. The lift of her shoulders, the tilt of her chin, the sparkle of her eyes all spelled a pride to which no one could deny her the right.

I turned back to Johnny Lingo after she had left.

"You admire her?" he asked.

"She...she's glorious," I said. "But she's not Sarita from Kiniwata."

"There's only one Sarita. Perhaps she does not look the way they say she looked in Kiniwata."

"She doesn't." The impact of the girl's appearance made me forget tact. "I heard she was homely. They all make fun of you because you let yourself be cheated by Sam Karoo."

"You think eight cows were too many?" A smile slid over his lips.

"No. But how can she be so different?"

"Do you ever think," he asked, "what it must mean to a woman to know that her husband settled on the lowest price for which she can be bought? And then later, when the women talk, they boast of what their husbands paid for them. One says four cows; another maybe six. How does she feel, the woman who was sold for one or two? This could not happen to my Sarita."

"Then you did this just to make her happy?" I asked.

"I wanted Sarita to be happy, yes. But I wanted more than that. You say she is different. This is true. Many things can change a woman. Things that happen inside; things that happen outside. But the thing that matters most is what she thinks about herself. In Kiniwata, Sarita believed she was worth nothing. Now she knows she is worth more than any other woman in the islands."

"Then you wanted…"

"I wanted to marry Sarita. I loved her and no other woman."

"But…"

"But," he finished softly, "I wanted an eight-cow wife."

LOOKING AHEAD...

Someone said, "We are not what we think we are. We are not even what others think we are. We are what we *think* others think we are." In other words, our estimation of our value as human beings is greatly influenced by the way people respond to us and the respect or disdain they reveal day by day. Those interactions shape our self-concepts and are translated into the nuances of our personalities.

Johnny Lingo was, indeed, a brilliant man. He was astute enough to know that his negotiations with Sarita's father would seal forever the self-concept of the woman he loved. That's why Sarita revealed such confidence and beauty. Let me say to the husbands and wives reading this book: *You* have the power to elevate or debase each other's self-esteem. Rather than tear down, don't miss a single opportunity to build up. For the next few evenings, we'll talk about how to do that.

JCD

FICKLE VALUES

I am fearfully and wonderfully made;
your works are wonderful, I know that full well.
Psalm 139:14

f I (JCD) were to draw a caricature of an adult experiencing a lifelong crisis of confidence, I would depict a bowed, weary traveler. Over his shoulder, I would place the end of a mile-long chain attached to tons of garbage. Inscribed on each piece of junk would be the details of some humiliation—a failure, a rejection, an embarrassment from the past. The traveler could let go of the chain, but he is convinced that he must drag that heavy load throughout life.

If this describes your own self-concept, realize that you can free yourself from the weight of your chain. You have judged yourself inferior based on shifting standards. In the 1920s, women asked plastic surgeons to *reduce* their breast size—now many women undergo surgery to do just the opposite. In King Solomon's biblical love song, the bride asked her groom to overlook her dark, well-tanned skin—but in our country today, she'd be the pride of the beach. Rembrandt painted overweight ladies, but now, "thin is in."

To be content with who we are as God's creations, we must base our self-image on His values, not on the fickle notions of human worth.

Just between us...

- Do you ever feel like the weary traveler described above?
- Do you sometimes feel that even God couldn't love you?
- What feelings of inferiority or inadequacy do you carry around? What would God say about your "junk"?
- Do I help to elevate your opinion of yourself, or am I part of the problem?

Lord, open our eyes to the half-truths and lies about ourselves that keep us in chains. We are made in Your image. May we affirm that beautiful truth in each other daily. Amen.

LOVE IN THE MIRROR

The Lord does not look at the things man looks at.
1 Samuel 16:7

he overemphasis on physical attractiveness in our society is frequently damaging to self-confidence. A case in point is the story of Peter Foster, a Royal Air Force pilot in World War II. During an air battle, Foster was the victim of a terrible fire. He survived, but his face was burned beyond recognition. He spent many anxious moments in the hospital wondering if his family—and especially his fiancée—would still accept him. They did. His fiancée assured him that nothing had changed except a few millimeters of skin. Two years later they were married.

Foster said of his wife, "She became my mirror. She gave me a new image of myself. When I look at her, she gives me a warm, loving smile that tells me I'm okay."

That's the way marriage ought to work, too—it should be a mutual admiration society that overlooks a million flaws and builds the self-esteem of both partners. Let's become each other's mirrors, reflecting back love and affirmation every chance we get.

Just between us...

- When was the last time I complimented you on your appearance?
- Is our marriage a "mutual admiration society"?
- Would you still love me if I became disfigured like Peter Foster?
- What do you think the Lord sees in me?
- How can I be a better "mirror" for you?

Lord Jesus, You came to bring Your presence and Your love to all—regardless of looks or ability, of health or condition. Thank You so much! May we reflect that same enthusiastic and unconditional love to each other in our marriage. Amen.

BODY AND SPIRIT

Don't be afraid; you are worth more than many sparrows.
Matthew 10:31

*I*n addition to society's obsession with physical beauty, women face other obstacles to maintaining confidence, including disrespect for wives and mothers who have chosen the traditional homemaking role. Furthermore, many wives, especially mothers of small children, feel isolated at home. Their husbands are physically and emotionally "elsewhere," pursuing careers, hobbies, or both. The result is often devastating, as women tend to derive their sense of self-worth from the emotional closeness achieved through relationships.

So what's the solution? We encourage you as the husband to be present with your wife in body and spirit. Set aside time for her. Listen to her. Romance her. Show her she's still your one-and-only sweetheart. On the other hand, don't expect to fill all of her emotional needs. Encourage her to develop meaningful friendships with other women and reach out to others in your community.

"Honor one another above yourselves." This simple phrase from the Bible (Romans 12:10) is the key to affirming the infinite worth of your spouse.

Just between us...

- (husband) When you're with other people, do you sometimes think, *They wouldn't like me if they really knew who I am?*
- (husband) Do you feel that I'm "present with you," or do I often seem preoccupied?
- (husband) What can I do to build your confidence this week?
- (husband) How can I support you in establishing friendships?

(husband) Dear God, thank You for the great worth You see in my wife. I see it, too, and I want to honor and cherish her more every day. Help me to bless her and make her strong in this way. Amen.

THE GREATEST GIFT

Consider the ravens: They do not sow or reap...yet God feeds them. And how much more valuable you are than birds!
Luke 12:24

lthough the battle for healthy self-confidence is most often fought by women, many men also struggle with the issue. Unlike a woman, a man derives his sense of worth primarily from the reputation he earns in his job or profession. He draws emotional satisfaction from achieving in business, becoming financially independent, developing a highly respected skill, being the "boss," or being loved and appreciated by his patients, clients, or business associates. When his career fails, however, look out. His confidence often falters, and he becomes vulnerable. Depression, anger, and withdrawal are just some of his potential responses.

Wives, here's something to remember: More than anything, your man needs your *respect*. Compliment him on the qualities you most admire in him. Avoid comments that debase or embarrass him—especially in the eyes of others. As much as is reasonably possible, understand and support his career, but also create such an affirming atmosphere at home that he will be happy to leave career concerns at the office.

The better you understand your differences, the more you'll appreciate the gift that is your mate.

Just between us...

- (wife) What achievement are you proudest of?
- (wife) Are you satisfied with the current state of your career?
- (wife) How can I help you with your career?
- (wife) How can I show more respect for you and what you do?

(wife) Father, thank You for my husband—for the energy, skills, and ambitions you've placed in him. Help him to know that You love him no matter how he performs, and please help me show him the honor and respect I feel. Amen.

DIVINE DECREE

God demonstrates his own love for us in this:
While we were still sinners, Christ died for us.

Romans 5:8

We've talked about the powerful influence others have on the way we see ourselves. Yet we should always remember that true value is granted by the One who created us in the first place. There is no greater sense of self-worth than knowing that He is acquainted with me personally; that He values me more than the possessions of the entire world; that He understands my fears and anxieties; that He reaches out to me when no one else cares; that He can turn my liabilities into assets and my emptiness into fullness; and that He has a place prepared for me—one where earthly pain and suffering will be but a dim memory. Indeed, the Lord of the universe places so much value on us that He gave His life to save us.

What a fantastic message of hope and encouragement for those who are broken and discouraged! This is self-worth at its richest—dependent not on the whims of birth or physical attractiveness or social judgment, but on the decree of our loving Lord.

Just between us...

* Do we base our self-image on the Lord's divine decree?
* What is it that really makes you feel valuable?
* Do I let you know often enough how much I value you?
* How can I better show how much I appreciate you?
* How can we remember that our worth as human beings is determined not by what we do or how we look or what we own, but by the fact that we are children of God?

Lord, we want so much to view ourselves and others from an eternal perspective. May we build our lives together on Your grand scheme, not on what is temporary and insignificant. Help us to live each day by the truth of Your divine decree. Amen.

A LITTLE GIRL, HIDING

You are a chosen people, a royal priesthood,
a holy nation, a people belonging to God.
1 Peter 2:9

I see a little girl skipping home from school in the late after-noon sun. Her dress is a hand-me-down intended for someone two sizes larger. Her shoes are unpolished, and her socks no longer have elastic around the top. She crosses a barren yard to reach her destination—a small house badly in need of paint and repair.

The walls inside the home are patched with brown butcher paper and paint to conceal where the little girl's father punched holes with his fist. The father frequently stumbles home in the middle of the night, smelling of alcohol, then wakes the little girl with shouts and threats against her mother. Sometimes the little girl hides from her father.

One day the little girl is driven home from a friend's birthday party. She asks to be let out in front of a clean house with a well-manicured lawn. She marches up the driveway and waves good-bye to her friends—but as soon as the car rounds the corner, she turns and walks several blocks to her real home. She's learned to hide her disgrace from others; on the inside, however, she feels ashamed, depressed, and worthless.

God, however, blesses the little girl. Her mother's wisdom and love sustain her. The mother insists that she attend church, where the little girl learns about Jesus and invites Him into her heart and life. When the little girl grows up and goes to college, she falls in love with a man who prom-ises to do his best to make her happy and build her up under God's direc-tion. And he does.

This story is deeply familiar to me because *I* was that little girl. Children who grow up in homes where they are loved and appreciated, where discipline and accountability are properly balanced with democ-racy and openness, develop a healthy sense of self-worth that usually car-ries into adulthood. But those of us who didn't experience this kind of childhood may need an extra dose of understanding from our marital partner. No matter what your spouse's background is, I pray you'll provide that support for the little boy or girl you're married to.

SMD

A Generous Spirit

R AGAMUFFIN B ROTHER

by Ron Mehl

*R*oy Angel was a dirt-poor preacher with a millionaire brother. Back in the oil boom days of the late 1940s, Roy's older brother happened to own the right piece of Texas prairie at the right time. When he sold, he became a multimillionaire overnight. Parlaying that good fortune, the elder Angel made some strategic investments in the stock market and then cashed in on several mushrooming business enterprises. He moved into the penthouse of a large apartment building in New York City and managed his investments from a posh Wall Street office.

A week before Christmas one year, the wealthy businessman visited his preacher-brother in Chicago and presented him with a new car—a gleaming, top-of-the-line Packard. Roy always kept his new car down the street in a parking garage, under the careful eye of an attendant. That's why when he came to get his Packard one morning, he was surprised to see a ragamuffin ghetto boy with his face pressed up against one of the car windows. The little boy wasn't doing anything suspicious; he was obviously just peering into the new car's interior with wide, admiring eyes.

"Hello, son," Roy said.

The boy spun around and looked at him. "Is this your car, mister?"

"Yes," Roy replied, "it is."

"How much did it cost?"

"Well, I really don't know."

The boy's face registered surprise. "You mean, you own this car, and you don't know how much it cost?"

"No, I don't—because my brother gave it to me. As a present."

At this the boy's eyes grew even wider. He thought for a moment, and then said wistfully, "I wish…I wish…."

Roy thought he knew how the boy would finish the sentence. He thought he was going to say, "I wish I had a brother like that."

But he didn't. The boy looked up at Roy and said, "I wish…I wish I could be a brother like that."

That intrigued the minister, and because those were more innocent times, he said, "Well, son, would you like to take a ride?"

The boy immediately replied, "You bet!"

So they got in the car together, exited the parking garage, and drove slowly down the street. The little boy ran his hand across the soft fabric of the front seat, inhaled the new-car smell, touched the shiny metal of the dashboard. Then he looked at his new friend and said, "Mister, would you—could you—take me by my house? It's just a few blocks from here."

Again, Roy assumed he knew what the lad had in mind. He thought the boy wanted to show off the car he was riding in to some of the neighborhood kids. He thought, *Well, why not?* So at his young passenger's direction, Roy pulled up in front of an old, run-down tenement building.

"Mister," the boy said as they stopped at the curb, "would you stay here just a minute? I'll be right back!"

Roy let the car idle as the boy rushed upstairs and disappeared.

After about ten minutes, the preacher began to wonder where the boy had taken himself. He got out of the car and looked up the unlighted stairwell. As he was looking up the dark stairs, he heard someone slowly coming down. The first thing he saw emerging from the gloom was two limp little legs. A moment later, Roy realized it was the little boy carrying an even smaller boy, evidently his younger brother.

The boy gently sat his brother down on the curb. "See?" he said with satisfaction. "It's just like I told you. It's a brand new car. His brother gave it to him, and someday I'm going to buy you a car just like that!"

LOOKING AHEAD...

In this story of two benevolent brothers, the millionaire certainly gave a nice present—but it's the little boy who is the better example of a generous spirit. How many children dream of giving a new car to their brother or sister? Somehow I get the feeling that this little fellow wouldn't squander a fortune if it came his way later in life.

During the coming week, we'll be talking about the incredible power of generosity for good—both inside our marriage and in our relationships with others. Tonight I leave you with a question: Do you have a generous spirit?

JCD

TIME AND WISDOM

For if the willingness is there, the gift is acceptable according
to what one has, not according to what he does not have.
2 Corinthians 8:12

enerosity comes in many forms. One version is material gifts. Another is the sharing of our time and wisdom. I (JCD) recall the example of one man who gave up two hours and influenced my life for years.

When I was in college, my aunt heard a speech by a well-known Christian psychologist, Dr. Clyde Narramore. "We need Christian young men and women in the field of mental health," Dr. Narramore said to the audience. "If you know of promising students who are interested, I'll be glad to meet with them." My aunt told me of this invitation, and I called Dr. Narramore for an appointment. He graciously agreed to see me, even though he was busy and didn't know me from Adam. As we talked in his living room, he laid out a plan for how I could become a psychologist. It's been over forty years since that conversation took place, yet I still remember the advice he gave me that day. It shaped the next five years of my life and helped channel me into a profession I love.

You may not have the financial means to help people in need, but you *can* offer them your time and insights. It may be just what they need to point them in the right direction.

Just between us...

- Who has influenced us through their gifts of time and wisdom?
- In what areas do we have expertise, insights, or available time that might help someone else?
- Who do we know who might benefit from our generosity?

Heavenly Father, tonight we reach for a truly generous life together. Guide and strengthen our willingness to share. Thank You for putting us on earth for something bigger and more meaningful than our own comfort or happiness. Amen.

"ARE YOU JESUS?"

Command them to do good, to be rich in good deeds,
and to be generous and willing to share.
1 Timothy 6:18

After their meeting ran late, five out-of-town salesmen hurried as fast as they could to catch their train. As they raced through the terminal, one inadvertently kicked over a slender table on which rested a basket of apples. It belonged to a ten-year-old blind boy who was selling apples to pay for his books and clothes for school. The salesmen clambered aboard the train, but one felt compassion for the boy. He asked his friends to call his wife and tell her he would be late getting home. Then he jumped off the train and returned to where the boy was standing.

As the salesman gathered up the apples scattered across the floor, he noticed that several were bruised or split. Reaching into his pocket, he said to the boy, "Here's twenty dollars for the apples we damaged. I hope we didn't spoil your day. God bless you." As he walked away, the boy called after him, "Are you Jesus?"

We are most like Christ when we show compassion and generosity to others. Jesus said, "Whatever you did for one of the least of these brothers of mine, you did for me" (Matthew 25:40). We reflect His character whether we're helping someone less fortunate or giving our mate a back rub at the end of the day.

Just between us...

- How do our interactions with others reflect the character of Jesus?
- When was the last time we stopped to help another person in need?
- How do you feel when you show compassion to someone else?

Lord, we ask that Your extravagant love would flow through us each day to touch those around us. Show us how to serve, to help, and to give without expecting anything in return. Amen.

SOMEONE IS LISTENING

[The righteous] are always generous and
lend freely; their children will be blessed.
Psalm 37:26

*B*e careful what you say in the presence of your babies. That's the advice of a researcher at Johns Hopkins University, who tells us that children only eight months of age are capable of hearing and remembering words, good and bad.

In a study by Dr. Peter Juscyzk, babies were exposed to three recorded stories for a period of about ten days. When they were tested in the lab two weeks later, they clearly recognized the words in the stories but failed to respond to those they hadn't heard. According to Robin Chapman, a University of Wisconsin language specialist, the study demonstrates that very young children attend to the sounds of language and are able to pick out those that are familiar. Chapman concludes that "a lot of language learning is happening in the first year of life."

Whether we like it or not, almost everything we say and do is observed and recorded—by the patrolman with a radar gun, by the convenience store video camera, and even by our young children. If our marriage models a spirit of generosity worth imitating, it will lead to blessings for everyone.

Just between us...

- What are some of your earliest memories of your parents' words and actions?
- If we videotaped ourselves, would we be pleased by what we saw?
- Besides each other, whom do we influence with our everyday words and deeds? Are we modeling a spirit of generosity for them?

Lord, we know that our every action has a tremendous impact on those around us, and we want to be mature, responsible and positive ambassadors for You. Help us glorify You in how we think, act, and speak. Amen.

SHOCKING WITH KINDNESS

So in everything, do to others what you would have
them do to you, for this sums up the Law and the Prophets.
Matthew 7:12

While standing in line at a grocery store checkout a few years ago, I (JCD) noticed that the elderly woman in front of me had filled her cart with more food than she could pay for. "I just don't understand where my money is," she said as she desperately searched the depths of her purse.

I whispered to the checker, "Total her bill, then accept whatever money she has, and put the rest on my bill." I paid an extra eight dollars to make up the difference. The old woman never knew I had helped her, but after she shuffled away, the checker had big tears in her eyes.

"I've been doing this work for twenty years," she said, "and I've never seen anyone do something like that before."

It was no big deal—an insignificant eight dollars—yet kind gestures are so rare today that many people find them shocking. As a husband and wife commissioned to demonstrate God's compassion to our world, we can make a tremendous impact through simple acts of kindness.

Just between us...

- What small kindness did I do for you this week that you appreciated?
- Am I treating you and others around us as kindly as I should?
- How does "shocking kindness" contribute to our witness for Christ?
- How can we be shockingly kind more often?

O Lord, Your kindness changed us forever. Your love broke into our lives most unexpectedly. Thank You so much! Empower us to love just like that. Amen.

A PITCHER'S DREAM

A generous man will prosper; he who
refreshes others will himself be refreshed.
Proverbs 11:25

*J*n 1985, Tim Burke achieved a lifelong dream—in fact, almost every boy's dream—when he signed to pitch for the Montreal Expos. He quickly proved his worth by setting a record for the most relief appearances by a rookie.

In the years that followed, Tim and his wife, Christine, adopted four children born with serious illnesses or defects. Neither Tim nor Christine was prepared for the tremendous demands such a family would bring. And with a grueling schedule, Tim was seldom around to help.

In 1993, only three months after signing a new, $600,000 contract, Tim decided to retire. When asked about his amazing decision, he said, "Baseball is going to do just fine without me. But I'm the only father my children have."

You might ask yourselves as a couple, "Does our current lifestyle, and our dreams and goals, fit with God's desire that we have a generous spirit?" Tim Burke's generous spirit caused him to give up his career dream, as well as the wealth it brought. Yet in the end, his act will be worth the sacrifice—his marriage and the well-being of four lives God placed in his care will reap eternal dividends. That's God's idea of a brilliant career move!

Just between us...

- Have you ever had to give up any of your dreams for someone?
- How do you feel now about those old dreams?
- What new dreams do you have for yourself and for us as a couple?
- How can we help each other achieve them?

Dear Lord, we surrender together whatever selfish dreams or ambitions are keeping us from the larger life You have in mind for us. Show us Your better idea. We want to do Your will with joy and expectation, because we trust You. Amen.

UNRESTRAINED GENEROSITY

"How great is the love the Father has lavished on us...!"

1 John 3:1

*I*t's no coincidence that we started this week's look at generosity with a story about a little boy. Children are often our best teachers.

Years ago during the week of my birthday, our family decided to go for a leisurely stroll through our local shopping center. Ryan, who was eight at the time, opened his piggybank and took out five dollars he had been saving for something special. As we walked along, window shopping and enjoying being together, Ryan announced that he wanted to have some time alone to go to the toy store and pet shop. We set a time and place where we would meet, and off he went. In about thirty minutes, he came walking up with a grin that stretched from ear to ear.

Ryan said, "Here, Mom, this is for your birthday. But you can open it right now!" By the look on his face, it was obvious that he felt strongly about my opening the gift right there in the middle of the mall. So we found a nearby bench. He announced his present had cost *a lot* of money. (He had spent the entire five dollars on it.)

As shoppers filed by, he watched excitedly while I carefully unwrapped the package. Gazing down at its contents, I was suddenly filled with emotion. His present wasn't anything he could have found in a toy or pet store. It wasn't even something you'd expect to receive from an eight-year-old boy. There in my lap was a lovely desk set. The ostrich-feathered white pen looked like an old-fashioned quill that Ben Franklin might have used to sign the Declaration of Independence. The stand was padded in matching white, with a spray of pink flowers delicately painted around the edges.

My eyes brimmed with tears as I hugged and thanked my son for such an extravagant gift. It has been many years since that day, and I still treasure that pen as a reminder of Ryan's spontaneous gift of love.

Most of us are too inclined to keep our purses or wallets shut tight against the opportunities for giving that are all around. Or when we give, we give what's convenient or interesting to *us*, not to the recipient.

In our marriages, we have so many chances to practice childlike, unrestrained generosity—with no ulterior motive, necessity, or expectation in mind. The more we give and receive that kind of love, the more we will experience the love of God in our homes. I think the apostle John had something like "unrestrained generosity" in mind when he wrote, "How great is the love the Father has lavished on us, that we should be called children of God! And that is what we are!" (1 John 3:1).

SMD

Seeing with God's Eyes

HI THERE!

by Nancy Dahlberg

One year our family spent the holidays in San Francisco with my husband's parents. Christmas was on a Sunday that year, and in order for us to be back at work on Monday, we had to drive the four hundred miles back home to Los Angeles on Christmas Day.

When we stopped for lunch in King City, the restaurant was nearly empty. We were the only family, and ours were the only children. I heard Erik, our one-year-old, squeal with glee: "Hi there. Hi there." He pounded his fat baby hands—whack, whack—on the metal tray of the high chair. His face was alive with excitement, eyes wide, gums bared in a toothless grin. He wriggled, chirped, and giggled. Then I saw the source of his merriment—and my eyes could not take it all in at once.

It was a man wearing a tattered rag of a coat, obviously bought eons ago, and dirty, greasy, worn pants. His toes poked out of used-to-be shoes, and his shirt had ring-around-the-collar all over. He had a face like none other—with gums as bare as Erik's.

"Hi there, baby," the disheveled man said. "Hi there, big boy. I see ya, buster."

My husband and I exchanged a look that was a cross between "What do we do?" and "Poor devil."

Our meal came, and the cacophony continued. Now the old bum was shouting from across the room: "Do you know patty-cake? Atta boy—do ya know peek-a-boo? Hey, look—he knows peek-a-boo!"

Erik continued to laugh and answer, "Hi there." Every call was echoed. Nobody thought it was cute. The guy was a drunk and a disturbance. I was embarrassed. My husband, Dennis, was humiliated. Even our six-year-old said, "Why is that old man talking so loud?"

As Dennis went to pay the check, he whispered for me to get Erik and meet him in the parking lot. *Lord, just let me out of here before he speaks to me or Erik,* I prayed as I bolted for the door.

It was soon obvious that both the Lord and Erik had other plans. As I drew closer to the man, I turned my back, trying to sidestep him—and any air he might be exhaling. As I did, Erik, with his eyes riveted on his new friend, leaned far over my arm and reached out with both hands in a baby's "pick me up" position.

In the split second of balancing my baby and turning to counter his weight, I came eye-to-eye with the old man. Erik was lunging for him, arms spread wide.

The bum's eyes both asked and implored, "Would you let me hold your baby?"

There was no need for me to answer because Erik propelled himself from my arms into the man's. Suddenly a very old man and very young baby clutched each other in a loving embrace. Erik laid his tiny head upon the man's ragged shoulder. The man's eyes closed, and I saw tears hover beneath his lashes. His aged hands—roughened by grime and pain and hard labor—gently, so gently, cradled my baby's bottom and stroked his back.

I stood awestruck. The old man rocked and cradled Erik in his arms for a moment, and then his eyes opened and set squarely on mine. He said in a firm, commanding voice, "You take care of this baby."

Somehow I managed to squeeze the words "I will" from a throat that seemed to have a stone lodged in it.

He pried Erik from his chest—unwillingly, longingly—as though he were in pain.

I held my arms open to receive my baby, and again the gentleman addressed me.

"God bless you, ma'am. You've given me my Christmas gift."

I could only mutter, "Thanks."

With Erik back in my arms, I hurried toward the car. Dennis wondered why I was crying and holding Erik so tightly and saying, "My God, my God, forgive me."

L O O K I N G   A H E A D...

Imagine for a moment viewing the world from a baby's perspective. Everything would fascinate you: the bright colors, the strange noises, and most certainly, the people. You'd want to touch, taste, and explore each one. Would you avert your eyes at the sight of a friendly bum? Of course not—even if he was toothless. Curious and trusting, you would return the bum's smile, then hold out your hands to give him a hug.

Babies see the world in a different light, don't they? They don't worry about what others think, and they don't prejudge others on the basis of appearance. Unfortunately, as adults we tend to go "blind"—to each other and to those around us—to what God is doing in our world. This week we'll talk about how we can learn to see in a fresh way—through God's loving eyes.

JCD

Believe the Best

If one falls down, his friend can help him up.

Ecclesiastes 4:10

The floor at Art and Naomi Hunt's house was scattered with wrenches, screwdrivers, and a host of oddly shaped pieces of wood and metal. The task at hand? To construct a new gas barbecue. Art knew that Naomi was the more mechanically gifted partner in their marriage, but he was determined to put together this latest addition to their arsenal of modern cooking appliances. As Art struggled, his wife watched. Finally, progress stopped altogether, and Art reluctantly asked for Naomi's advice. But instead of just giving her opinion, Naomi took the wrench from Art's hand and began finishing the job herself.

Not surprisingly, Art felt rather emasculated, incompetent, and foolish. Now he faced a choice. He could believe either the best or the worst about Naomi's actions. If he believed the worst, he would think, *Man, she's taking control. She doesn't have any confidence in my abilities.* Or, believing the best, he could tell himself, *She's going further than I asked her to, but she's just trying to help me. That's okay.* Art chose the latter.

In a lifelong relationship, we regularly arrive at these emotional crossroads. We could go either way: give our partner the benefit of the doubt, or give ourselves the right to take offense. When we choose to see our spouse's good intentions and base our reactions on them, we're taking the road toward intimacy and away from unnecessary conflict. As Art Hunt understood, the real task at hand was building his relationship with Naomi, not putting together a new gadget.

Just between us...

- How do we usually react when one of us steps in to help the other?
- Do we see the best in each other's motives? If not, why?
- Do either of us give the other reason to question our motives?

Dear God, my spouse is Your gift to me, and I'm grateful. Help me to always believe, see, and act on the best. Grant me grace to mature in this area. Amen.

SPLIT VISION

A wise man's heart guides his mouth.
Proverbs 16:23

*I*sn't it curious how in the midst of a nasty family argument we can shake our bad mood the instant the telephone rings or a neighbor knocks on the door? Have you ever been brought up short by a small voice questioning such a sudden turn to peaches and cream after twenty minutes of fire and brimstone? Sometimes we treat those we love the worst, and kids are quick to recognize this hypocrisy.

Mark Hatfield, a longtime senator from Oregon and the father of four, said his wife once stung him by saying, "I just wish you were as patient with your children as you are with your constituents." He isn't alone. We're all guilty at times of what might be called "split vision"— treating acquaintances with forbearance while losing patience or even heaping contempt on those under our own roof. We assume the worst. We pounce on every shortcoming. We never miss an opportunity to harangue. In the process, we wound the people we care about most.

It's time we cut one another a little slack at home. If we say our spouses, children, and parents are the most significant people in our lives, we can prove it by showing them the same kindnesses we would bestow on our most honored guests.

Just between us...

- Are we as patient with each other at home as we are with guests and strangers?
- Why do you think we can be so hard on each other?
- How can we encourage each other to avoid this kind of "split vision"?

Father, open our eyes to see one another the way You do. Forgive us for the laziness and selfishness that so easily sour our family relationships. Help us guard our words and actions so that we may be pleasing in Your sight. Amen.

WANDERING SHEEP

"If a man owns a hundred sheep, and one of them
wanders away, will he not leave the ninety-nine...
and go to look for the one that wandered off?"
Matthew 18:12

*I*f you are parents of small children, you know exactly how the shepherds mentioned in the Bible felt as they watched over their flocks. Even for a mother with "eyes in the back of her head," keeping one active child from wandering off can seem as big a challenge as corralling a hundred sheep!

Jesus is called a shepherd, too, but His flock is all of humanity and He watches over us day and night. That's why He called Himself the Good Shepherd. He came to earth to die so that not one soul would have to be lost. During His earthly ministry, He was always on the lookout for lost souls. He stayed up late to talk to Nicodemus (John 3:2). He wouldn't let Zacheus hide unnoticed in a tree (Luke 19:5). And when the Pharisees were about to stone a despised adulteress, Jesus intervened with a message of forgiveness and direction—"Go, and sin no more" (John 8:11).

Every day, we have divine appointments to lead others into God's flock—not just our family, friends, neighbors, and coworkers, but also people we've never met before and may never see again. God's wisdom and power are at our disposal. We just have to keep our eyes open.

Just between us...

- Do you see Jesus as your Good Shepherd? Why or why not?
- As a couple, are we watching for "lost sheep"?
- How can we be more watchful for opportunities to reach unbelievers?
- Is there anyone "lost" with whom we can talk this week?

Lord Jesus, show us how to demonstrate Your great love and compassion to those around us. We, too, want to be shepherds of lost souls. Amen.

No Junk Allowed

"Man looks at the outward appearance,
but the LORD looks at the heart."

1 Samuel 16:7

*S*even-year-old Chris Krebs was born with cerebral palsy and was profoundly retarded. One day he and his father, Greg, sat in a hospital lounge waiting for Mrs. Krebs, who worked at the hospital. Another man, shabbily dressed and emanating a peculiar aroma, was also waiting there. He looked like a bum or derelict. Greg went to the nurses' station and asked how much longer his wife would be. When he returned, he saw Chris sitting by the man. The man was sobbing, and Greg wondered what Chris had done to disturb him.

"I'm sorry if my son offended you," Greg said.

The man replied, "Offended me? Your son is the only person who has hugged me in the last twenty years!" Greg later said, "I realized at that moment Chris had a more Christlike love for this man than I did."

Although disrespect for the disabled or less fortunate is characteristic of our culture, we know there is no "junk" in God's value system. He loves every one of us the same. He sees our potential, and He uses each person to accomplish some part of His purpose. As His children, we're called to look at everyone through the lens of His perfect love.

When we show compassion and respect to the people who cross our paths from day to day, we are also likely to treat our spouse the same way. It all begins with a spirit of loving-kindness.

Just between us...

- Has anyone ever unexpectedly modeled Christ's love to you?
- How can we encourage each other to see value and potential in everyone we meet?

Father, may we always be sensitive to the needs and value of other people.
Help us to share Your love to them, no matter who they are. Amen.

IF ONLY

*We were under great pressure, far beyond our ability
to endure.... But this happened that we might not
rely on ourselves but on God.*

2 Corinthians 1:8–9

*I*n my (JCD's) book *When God Doesn't Make Sense,* I wrote about the burdensome situations in life that we can't understand. Some are painful or life-threatening, others are simply inconvenient or uncomfortable. We know that God could eliminate these problems with a whisper, but, instead, He allows us to struggle.

Why? One of His greater purposes is to reveal His power to us. This understanding comes straight from the apostle Paul who wrote, "But we have this treasure in earthen vessels [clay pots], that the excellency of the power may be of God, and not of us" (2 Corinthians 4:7, KJV).

Instead of accepting the irritations of life, many people struggle with what I call the "if onlys." *"If only* I didn't have diabetes (or deafness or sinus infections)." *"If only* I were not infertile." *"If only* I hadn't gotten into that bad business relationship (or lawsuit or loveless marriage)." *"If only* we didn't have a sick child." *"If only* we weren't so strapped financially."

Are you struggling with "if onlys" today? If so, we encourage you to release them to God. He has a perfect, loving plan for all of your life—even when life seems less than ideal. We may not see why God allows hardship in our lives, but we can be assured it is part of His eternal plan for our good. He asks us to accept His love and reach in humble dependence for *His* sufficiency.

Just between us...

- Have we become discouraged by "if onlys" in our lives?
- Can we learn to depend on the Lord at this point of need?
- Has God been able to use our "if onlys" for His purposes?

Lord, help us rely on Your great love for us even when we feel weighed down by disappointments. Comfort and strengthen us in our need. Amen.

LOOKING OUT FOR THE SINGLE MOM

Look after orphans and widows in their distress.

James 1:27

*M*any years ago I was working around the house when a knock came at the door. When I opened it, there stood Sally, a young woman in her late teens. "I'm selling brushes," she said, "and I wonder if you'd like to buy any." I told her politely that I wasn't interested in buying anything that day, and Sally said, "I know. No one else is, either." With that, she began to cry.

I invited Sally to come in for a cup of coffee and asked her to share her story. It turned out that she was an unmarried mother who was struggling mightily to support her two-year-old son. That night, we went to her shabby little apartment above a garage to see how we could help her and her toddler. When we opened the cupboards, there was nothing there for them to eat—I mean nothing. That night they both dined on a can of Spaghetti-Os. We took Sally to the market and did what we could to help her get on her feet.

There are millions of single mothers out there who are desperately trying to survive in a hostile world. All of them could use a little kindness—from babysitting to providing a meal to repairing the washing machine to just showing a little thoughtfulness. Have you opened your eyes to them lately?

Raising kids all alone is the toughest job in the universe. Look around your neighborhood through "God's eyes." Is a single mom going down for the third time? How about giving a helping hand? Not only will she be encouraged, but her children will bless you as well.

SMD

"And Then We Had Kids"

SURPRISE, SURPRISE, SURPRISE!

by Philip Gulley

y wife and I waited eight years to have children. I was in college, then graduate school, and I thought I was too busy. My mother had five children in seven years, was principal of a school, and attended college all at the same time. And she did a good job, which I point out to her every Saturday when I visit her at the Home for the Mentally Distraught.

Despite our childless state, my wife and I were willing, indeed eager, to share our perspective on child-rearing with anyone who would listen. Now that we have children, we seldom offer advice. The moment you tell other parents how to raise their kid, the odds increase that your own child will turn up on America's Most Wanted.

So we don't give advice anymore, because we've realized we don't know anything about children. Before we had children, we knew everything. Now we have children, and the only parent we feel superior to is Ma Barker.

It's been hard to admit my ignorance about child-rearing. It's easy to be smug when you're driving home from someone else's house saying, "When I have children, they will never act like that." Now when our childless friends visit, I tell them when they leave, "Don't talk about us on your way home." They know what I mean.

Most experiences don't turn out the way we'd planned. Parenting is one of them.

Take Spencer's second Christmas. Someone in the church gave him a nativity set as a gift. He was particularly taken with the wise men, one of whom he used as tableware. He dipped Balthasar up to his ears in ketchup and licked him clean. My wife said, "Honey, don't dip the wise man in the ketchup."

There are many things we anticipated telling our children—things like, "Because I said so, that's why!" and "Not in this house you won't!" and even "Don't put that in the toilet!" But we never imagined ourselves saying, "Don't dip the wise man in the ketchup."

That's the kick about life. We think we have it figured out, but then we wade in and discover otherwise. Kind of like Gomer Pyle used to say, "Surprise, surprise, surprise!"

All in all, this is a good thing. For when our future is sure and certain, when all the corners are tucked in nice and neat, there is no need for faith.

Consider King David. He grew up a shepherd, which was nothing to write home about. If a dog can do your job, it's time to worry. So David grew up a shepherd, but he died a king. Goes to show we never know what direction life will take.

This is especially true of being a parent. We never know everything there is to know. The only solution is to do your best and trust God for the rest. At least that's what my sainted mother used to tell me, back in my younger days when I knew it all.

LOOKING AHEAD...

Is there any endeavor that husbands and wives are less adequately prepared for than parenting? The task of raising a child is daunting, exhausting, frustrating, discouraging, humbling—and just to keep it interesting, it comes with an unexpected twist around every corner. Yet when guided by dedication and prayer, parenting is also the most fulfilling and wonderful experience in living. And it doesn't *have* to be as chaotic as Phil Gulley's tongue-in-cheek description makes it out to be.

Those of you who are parents already realize that you will make mistakes and that you'll never know it all. But nothing worth accomplishing comes easy anyway, and it's the very challenge of child rearing that makes success so satisfying. This week we're going to talk about how to make the most of the experience.

JCD

JUST WAITIN' FOR YOU, DAD

In you our fathers put their trust;
they trusted and you delivered them.
Psalm 22:4

husband and wife on vacation at a lake didn't notice their three-year-old son Billy wandering toward the dock to investigate a boat. He tried to stretch his short legs from the dock to the boat, but didn't quite make it—and fell into six-feet-deep water. The splash brought Dad running. He dove into the murky water, groping with his arms and legs trying to find Billy. His lungs nearly bursting, he pushed toward the surface—and touched Billy, whose arms were locked around a piling four feet underwater. Dad pried him loose, and they hit the surface together, gasping for air.

When they had recovered, Dad asked little Billy what he was doing hanging onto that piling. Billy's answer: "Just waitin' for you, Dad."

When his life was on the line, Billy knew his dad would come through. It's true that fathers bear heavy responsibility for the welfare and protection of their children. We parents have a tough assignment, but most of us wouldn't have it any other way. The most difficult, important, and wonderful task of all is to teach our kids to trust their heavenly Father even more than they depend on Dad.

Just between us...

- Did you as a child ever have a close call like Billy's? Was your father there for you?
- Are we teaching our kids to depend on the Lord?
- How can we learn to trust God as much as Billy trusted his dad?

Father, we praise You that You are strong and trustworthy at all times. We say with the psalmist—"The LORD is the stronghold of my life—of whom shall I be afraid?" May our words, attitudes, and behavior model complete trust in You as a way of life in our home. Amen.

BALLOONS AND CHILDREN

"My time has not yet come."
John 2:4

I (JCD) once attended a wedding in a beautiful garden setting. After the minister told the groom to kiss the bride, about 150 colorful, helium-filled balloons were released into the blue sky. Within a few seconds the balloons were scattered, some rising hundreds of feet overhead and others cruising toward the horizon. A few balloons struggled to clear the upper branches of the trees, while the showoffs became mere pinpoints of color in the sky.

Like balloons, some boys and girls are born with more helium than others. They soar effortlessly to the heights, while others wobble dangerously close to the trees. Their frantic folks run along underneath, huffing and puffing to keep them airborne.

Are you a parent of a low-flying child? Over the years, I've worked with hundreds of families whose children were struggling in one way or another. Based on what I've seen, let me pass along a word of encouragement to worried parents: *Sometimes the child who has the most trouble getting off the ground eventually reaches the greatest height!*

Just between us...

- What kinds of balloons do our kids most resemble?
- Do we tend to panic when our low-fliers drift in the wrong direction?
- Do we love them any less than those who soar?
- How can we avoid prematurely judging how a child will turn out?
- How can we pump more "helium" into our relationship with our low-flier?

Heavenly Father, tonight we ask for wisdom and patience as we raise our children. We let go of our own requirements and timelines for their lives. We trust Your providence and grace. Every day, help us obey You in this great calling of being a parent. Amen.

A TALE OF TWO HOMES

"If a house is divided against itself,
that house cannot stand."
Mark 3:25

*O*uppose that you're seven years old. You arrive home from school, and your mother welcomes you with a smile and a snack. Later your father comes home. Mom and Dad greet each other with a kiss and loving words. Dad gives you a warm hug. That night, after you finish your homework, the three of you enjoy a family game. Finally, you say your prayers and fall asleep.

Now put yourself in another seven-year-old's place. You come home from school to a mother who, when she's home at all, is on the phone or watching television. You eat a bag of candy by yourself. Later your father returns. Mom complains about the unfinished garage project. Dad replies angrily and walks past you to the kitchen. You watch television all evening, then crawl into bed and fall asleep listening to your parents argue.

One home is safe and nurturing; the other lonely and contentious. Too often, children grow up in homes like the latter—or worse. So ask yourself: Which scenario best describes your family? Further, how would you describe the mood of your household? Divided or united? Amiable or argumentative? Supportive or sarcastic? Every day, the story of your home is etching itself into the spirit and memory of your children.

Just between us...

- How does the way we were brought up affect the mood in our household today?
- How do you think our children would describe our home?
- How can we make sure our home is a positive environment?

Loving Lord, we know that our relationship sets the tone for our children's growing-up experience. Help us make our marriage the starting point of a good home and of a happy, Christ-honoring childhood for our kids. Amen.

THE BOTTOM LINE

Train a child in the way he should go,
and when he is old he will not turn from it.

Proverbs 22:6

*T*he contradictory advice given in popular culture about what children need is enough to drive a conscientious parent to distraction. In days past, moms and dads learned child-rearing from their parents, who learned from theirs. Rightly or wrongly, they had a sense of confidence about what they were doing. That's because the traditional approach to parenting boils down to some very basic ideas. Here are just a few:

—When your children ask, "Who's in charge?" tell them.

—When they mutter, "Who loves me?" take them in your arms and surround them with affection.

—When they defiantly challenge you, win decisively. Talk to them. Set up clear boundaries and then enforce the rules firmly and fairly.

—Expose your children to interesting things. Help them use their time wisely.

—Raise them in a stable family with two parents who love each other and enjoy a strong marriage.

—Teach them to love the Lord and understand His Word.

—Treat them with respect and dignity and expect the same in return.

—Set aside time to build friendship and love between generations.

Then enjoy the sweet benefits of competent parenthood and a wonderful family!

Just between us...

• How are we doing on this list of parenting basics?

• Where do we see progress? Which ones need special attention?

Father, thank You for the timeless wisdom that we can follow to help us raise our children right. May we parent wisely and lovingly, trusting in Your blessing. Amen.

STAY THE COURSE

*"Let the little children come to me, and do not hinder them,
for the kingdom of God belongs to such as these."*

Mark 10:14

*I*f we believe that the eternal souls of our children hang in the balance, why would we take a casual approach to parenting? If our eyes are fully opened to this awesome assignment, why would we ignore and neglect so great an opportunity?

The Good News provides the *only* satisfactory explanation for why we're here and where we're going. When we accept our spiritual responsibility as parents, our entire family is likely to follow our example into eternity: "Believe in the Lord Jesus, and you will be saved—you and your household" (Acts 16:31).

Are you the parents of young children or a houseful of teenagers? We understand how difficult it is for you to keep this eternal perspective in mind as you race through your days. We encourage you not to let yourselves become discouraged with the responsibility of parenting. Yes, it is incredibly difficult, and at times you'll feel like throwing in the towel. But we beg you to stay the course! Get on your knees before the Lord and ask for His strength and wisdom. Finish the job to which He has called you!

There is no more important task in this life.

Just between us...

- Can we be more intentional in introducing our children to Jesus Christ?
- How can we keep eternal priorities foremost in our minds?
- Is there a pressing need we can pray about together tonight?

Lord, nothing will count more in eternity than that we've been faithful parents who have helped usher our children into Your presence. Give us strength and wisdom for this task. By Your Spirit, draw our children to You. Amen.

LETTING GO

Bring [your children] up in the training
and instruction of the Lord.
Ephesians 6:4

I admit that it was difficult to watch my two children, Danae and Ryan, grow up. I knew they couldn't remain children forever, and I certainly didn't want to freeze their development. But I loved every minute of their childhood, and I cherish the memories we created.

I worked especially hard on "letting go" of Danae during her last three years at home. One of the most difficult times occurred when she was fifteen. She was having trouble getting ready for school on time, and I repeatedly rescued her by driving her there at the last minute. Finally, Jim and I agreed that it was time for Danae to accept full responsibility for beating the tardy bell.

One morning Danae missed her carpool ride, and she appeared at my door as I was preparing for an appointment. I ignored her hints about driving her, and we lived too far from school for her to walk. When she realized I wasn't going to rescue her, she called Dial-A-Ride, our city-sponsored cab company. She gathered her books and sat on the curb in front of our house with her head down, waiting for the cab.

I reluctantly faced one of my most difficult assignments ever. I backed my car out of the driveway and drove off, leaving my beloved teenage daughter dejected and alone. My mind flooded with all the horrible things that could happen to a young girl by herself. I asked God to protect Danae and help her learn from this experience.

The Lord heard my prayer. Danae came bounding into the house after school, threw her books on the table, and wailed, "Oh, Mother! How embarrassing! Do you know what kind of cab Dial-A-Ride has? It is a huge, old, beat-up station wagon. The driver drove me right up in front of the school, and all my friends saw me. Oh, I will never do that again!" The next morning, Danae was up at the crack of dawn.

It's extremely difficult for loving, caring parents to let their vulnerable children face embarrassment or failure. Our impulse is to bail them out or cover for their irresponsibility. But if we have faith in our objectives—and in our kids—we'll stay the course and all do some growing up together.

SMD

The Divorce "Solution"

DEAR DADDY

by Gary Smalley and John Trent

Largely unused in marriages, homes, friendships, and businesses is a tool called *emotional word pictures* that can supercharge communication and change lives. This concept is as old as ancient kings but so timeless that it has been used throughout the ages in every society. It has the capacity to capture people's attention by simultaneously engaging their thoughts and feelings. Along with its ability to move us to deeper levels of intimacy, it has the staying power to make a lasting impression.

When faced with the breakup of her parents' marriage, a hurting teenager named Kimberly used the following word picture in this letter to her father:

Dear Daddy,

It's late at night, and I'm sitting in the middle of my bed writing to you. I've wanted to talk with you so many times during the past few weeks. But there never seems to be any time when we're alone.

Dad, I realize you're dating someone else. And I know you and Mom may never get back together. That's terribly hard to accept—especially knowing that you may never come back home or be an "everyday" dad to me and Brian again. But I want you at least to understand what's going on in our lives.

Don't think that Mom asked me to write this. She didn't. She doesn't know I'm writing, and neither does Brian. I just want to share with you what I've been thinking.

Dad, I feel like our family has been riding in a nice car for a long time. You know, the kind you always like to have as a company car. It's the kind that has every extra inside and not a scratch on the outside.

But over the years, the car has developed some problems. It's smoking a lot, the wheels wobble, and the seat covers are ripped. The car's been really hard to drive or ride in because of all the shaking and squeaking. But it's still a great automobile—or at least it could be. With a little work, I know it could run for years.

Since we got the car, Brian and I have been in the backseat while you and Mom have been up front. We feel really secure with you driving and Mom beside you. But last month, Mom was at the wheel.

It was nighttime, and we had just turned the corner near our house. Suddenly, we all looked up and saw another car, out of control, heading straight for us. Mom tried to swerve out of the way, but the other car smashed into us. The impact sent us flying off the road and crashing into a lamppost.

The thing is, Dad, just before we were hit, we could see that you were driving the other car. And we saw something else: Sitting next to you was another woman.

It was such a terrible accident that we were all rushed to the emergency ward. But when we asked where you were, no one knew. We're still not really sure where you are or if you were hurt or if you need help.

Mom was really hurt. She was thrown into the steering wheel and broke several ribs. One of them punctured her lungs and almost pierced her heart.

When the car wrecked, the back door smashed into Brian. He was covered with cuts from the broken glass, and he shattered his arm, which is now in a cast. But that's not the worst. He's still in so much pain and shock that he doesn't want to talk or play with anyone.

As for me, I was thrown from the car. I was stuck out in the cold for a long time with my right leg broken. As I lay there, I couldn't move and didn't know what was wrong with Mom and Brian. I was hurting so much myself that I couldn't help them.

There have been times since that night when I wondered if any of us would make it. Even though we're getting a little better, we're all still in the hospital. The doctors say I'll need a lot of therapy on my leg, and I know they can help me get better. But I wish it were you who was helping me, instead of them.

The pain is so bad, but what's even worse is that we all miss you so much. Every day we wait to see if you're going to visit us in the hospital, and every day you don't come. I know it's over. But my heart would explode with joy if somehow I could look up and see you walk into my room.

At night when the hospital is really quiet, they push Brian and me into Mom's room, and we all talk about you. We talk about how much we loved driving with you and how we wish you were with us now.

Are you all right? Are you hurting from the wreck? Do you need us like we need you? If you need me, I'm here and I love you.

Your daughter,
Kimberly

LOOKING AHEAD...

More than two months before writing this letter, Kimberly had watched her father, Steve, walk out of his family's life with plans to divorce his wife and pursue a relationship with another woman. The heartache that Kimberly, her mother, and her brother felt was indescribable. But the anguish also extended to Steve. Only a few weeks after leaving, he began to second-guess his decision.

That's the impact of divorce. It appears to be a solution when in fact it brings only pain and new difficulties.

A few days after receiving Kimberly's letter, Steve appeared on his family's doorstep and asked to come back. He realized that divorce wasn't the answer to his family's problems. Would you ever consider it an answer to yours? Has your marriage ever been on the brink of breaking up? This week, we're going to take a candid look at the divorce "solution."

JCD

TAKING THE PLUNGE

A wife must not separate from her husband. But if she does, she must remain unmarried or else be reconciled to her husband.
1 Corinthians 7:10–11

*D*ivorce often looks like a "quick fix" for an unpleasant situation, but it is usually far more painful than advertised. Contemplating those on the verge of taking this drastic step brings to mind a documentary film made during the early days of motion pictures. It shows a self-styled inventor near the top of the Eiffel Tower with a pair of homemade wings strapped to his arms. He paces back and forth, trying to work up the courage to jump. If the wings work, he'll be famous. If they fail, he'll fall to his death. Finally the "flier" climbs on the rail, wobbles for a moment, then jumps—and drops like a rock.

Depressed and hurting spouses who choose divorce are like that hapless man on the Eiffel Tower. They feel that they can't go back, and they're enticed forward by the lure of freedom—of soaring away, leaving the pain and disappointment behind. So they jump...only to find themselves tumbling headlong into custody battles, loneliness, bitterness, and even poverty. In time, the long-term cost of their decision becomes clear. Some again see their mate's good qualities, but by then it's too late. They've already taken the plunge.

Just between us...

- When have you jumped into a situation that you later regretted?
- Has Scripture ever helped you avoid such a mistake? When?
- What is the attraction, and danger, of "quick fix" solutions in marriage?
- Why do you think God commands us to avoid divorce?

Lord of married lovers, You have called us to commitment. When forsaking our covenant seems easier than staying, grant us courage. Help us to recognize the deceitfulness of the divorce "solution." Protect our marriage from every harm, including our own short-sightedness. Amen.

DIVORCE AND KIDS

And a husband must not divorce his wife.
1 Corinthians 7:11

*T*he daughter in Sunday's "Dear Daddy" story described the trauma of her father's deserting their family as like being in a car wreck. That is the impact divorce typically has on children. It is devastating!

For more than twenty-five years, California psychologist Judith Wallerstein has tracked hundreds of children of divorce from childhood to adulthood. She's found that the distress young children experience after a divorce remains with them throughout their lives, making it more difficult for them to cope with challenges. "Unlike the adult experience," Wallerstein says, "the child's suffering does not reach its peak at the breakup and then level off. The effect of the parents' divorce is played and replayed throughout the first three decades of the children's lives." Harvard University psychiatrist Armand Nicholi says that the pain of divorce is worse for children five years later than at the time the family disintegrates. He also links interruption of parent-child relationships with an escalation in psychiatric problems for children.

The next time the idea of divorce enters your thoughts, consider the consequences of such an act on the most vulnerable members of your family. Research shows that time doesn't heal those wounds.

Just between us...

- Do you agree with the statements of these mental health professionals?
- If your parents divorced, what was your experience during and after the breakup?
- What would happen to our kids (or future children) if we divorced?

Father, we thank You for the tender lives You've placed in our care. We resolve never to harm them through the violence of divorce. Strengthen and bless this commitment in our thoughts and actions each day. Amen.

HAZARDOUS TO YOUR HEALTH

So guard yourself in your spirit, and do not
break faith with the wife of your youth.
Malachi 2:15

*W*riter Pat Conroy, after telling his three daughters that he and his wife were divorcing, said he felt like he had "doused my entire family with gasoline and struck a match." The painful effects resulting from such stress and guilt are not just a temporary problem. Dr. David Larson, a Washington, D.C., psychiatrist and researcher, has observed that all types of cancer strike divorced individuals more frequently than married people. He has also noted that premature death rates are significantly higher among divorced people and that being divorced and a nonsmoker is only slightly less hazardous than staying married and smoking a pack or two a day.

In the 1960s, the surgeon general declared cigarettes harmful to the smoker's health. More recently, researchers have warned us about the dangers of foods high in fat and cholesterol. Perhaps it's time someone issued a warning about the health risks of marital conflict. Ripping "one flesh" apart is one of the most devastating experiences in life. There *must* be a better way to deal with conflict.

Just between us...

- Is the state of our marriage affecting our health?
- How is divorce hazardous to a person's spiritual life? (See Malachi 2:13–16.)
- What can we do this week to promote our physical and emotional health?

Dear God, we receive this reminder that the damage done by broken marriages extends to the body, mind, and spirit. We humbly ask for Your help to make divorce "not an option" for our future. Amen.

NO FAULT?

Anyone who divorces his wife, except for marital
unfaithfulness, and marries another woman commits adultery.

Matthew 19:9

One reason divorce has become so common today is the advent of "no-fault" divorce laws, first introduced in California in 1969. Over the following fifteen years, every state in America adopted some form of no-fault legislation. And to what result? According to the *Statistical Abstract of the United States,* since these laws began taking effect the number of divorces in this country has increased 279 percent.

In essence, no-fault divorce has nullified the sacredness of marriage in the eyes of the law, making it an unenforceable contract. A man and woman can abandon their family more easily than they can abrogate almost any other agreement that bears their signature. In terms of the law, it matters not that they've made a solemn promise before God, friends, relatives, a member of the clergy, or a licensed representative of the state.

However, no matter how easy the laws make it to get a divorce, it will always remain infinitely difficult to repair the damage.

Just between us...

- What would you say to the couple who insist, "Our divorce is nobody's fault. We just didn't get along, so we're going our separate ways"?
- Do we know anyone who has sought a divorce, only to regret the move?
- Are we committed to staying together, even through tough times?

Lord, the courts have made it so easy to tear apart that which You have bound together. Forgive us, forgive our land, and bring us to repentance. Help us keep Your commands as the ultimate law of our marriage and family. Amen.

THE SECOND TIME AROUND

"I will forgive their wickedness and
will remember their sins no more."
Jeremiah 31:34

any of you reading these discussions about the consequences of divorce have already taken that fateful step—
willingly or not—and then remarried. You may also be
facing the unique challenge of raising children from two sets of parents.
We assure you that it has not been our intention to heap additional guilt
on you. We have a loving God who offers forgiveness to those who truly
seek His will. Only He knows the condition of your spiritual "heart" and
the circumstances that led to the end of your first marriage. If you have
not dealt with those matters before God, we urge you to do so tonight.

Our hope is that you will reaffirm the sanctity of your present marriage and fight to preserve it with all your heart and soul. With the Lord's
help, you can still forge a marriage that lasts a lifetime. We encourage you
to learn from the mistakes of your previous relationships, rely wholeheartedly on God's principles for marriage, and make the firm decision
that *nothing* will tear you away from your mate.

Remember, there are no second-class members of God's family. God
still wants to give you His best. And as you seek Him together, He will.

Just between us...

- What would be (or is) most difficult about a second marriage?
- Is God willing to forgive those who divorce for the wrong reasons?
- What do you think is the most painful part of a divorce? How can
  we use this information to keep our marriage strong?

Father, forgive our sins and selfish mistakes. We cast all our hopes for our mar-
riage on Your truths, and together we wholeheartedly seek to obey Your will
for us. Thank You for Your mercies, which are new every morning. Amen.

MANY TROUBLES

"I hate divorce," says the LORD God of Israel.
Malachi 2:16

Who would know better than the architect of marriage that living with another person day in and day out isn't always easy? God understands what we're going through, even in our worst circumstances. When Paul stated that "those who marry will face many troubles in this life" (1 Corinthians 7:28), he wasn't kidding!

Fortunately, God has given us a blueprint in Scripture for success and fulfillment in our marriage relationship. The Lord designed marriage for our benefit, and He knows that destroying this partnership is harmful to us in countless ways.

No wonder God hates divorce. He has made it clear that the concept of separating permanently from one's marriage partner is not only unacceptable, but abhorrent. The only exception He has recorded for us is in the case of adultery, and even in that situation there is room for forgiveness and reconciliation if we follow Christ's merciful example.

Our encouragement to you as a husband and wife who seek God's best is a very personal one. As Jim and I have sought out and followed the Word of God, *we have found all the stability and fulfillment in our marriage that He has promised!* And you will, too. Marriage is His idea, after all, and His principles and values naturally produce harmony between people. It's sinful behaviors that kill a relationship.

When your time of "many troubles" strikes, Satan will be ready at just the right moment to suggest the "solution" of divorce. Perhaps you've already arrived at this place in the past. Surely you know and love couples who have come to this moment, and have chosen to believe Satan's lie.

My prayer is that you will believe God instead.

SMD

A Time to Laugh

What about Bob?

by Phil Callaway

hanksgiving weekend began the way Bob and Audrey Meisner had planned. Piling a full-size van high with mattresses, sleeping bags, and children, they drove a thousand miles through the flatlands of Manitoba to the in-laws in Michigan. It was a beautiful trip. Patchwork prairies sprinkled with lakes stretched toward the horizon. Bare poplar branches held up their arms in surrender to winter. The children counted columns of Canadian geese deserting their homeland and heading for Florida. Neither Bob nor Audrey knew that the beauty of the first leg of their trip would stand in sharp contrast to the journey home.

The weekend was filled with relatives, turkey, and laughter. On Sunday night the Meisners said their good-byes and headed for home. Leaving at 11:00 P.M., they drove through the night, arriving in Minneapolis about 8:30 the next morning. Though Mom and Dad were tired, the Mall of America beckoned, and it was many hours before they watched the skylines of the Twin Cities disappear in the rearview mirror as they drove toward the setting sun.

When Audrey offered to drive, Bob clambered into the back of the van, where he disappeared behind some sleeping bags and drifted off to sleep.

An hour and a half later, Audrey pulled into a rest stop as quietly as she could, hoping the family would sleep on. As she let the engine idle, she noticed how it seemed to be missing a cylinder, which made her think of Bob's snoring coming from the back of the van.

After using the restroom, Audrey climbed back into the van, stirred some coffee, took a long sip, and pulled back onto the freeway. Two hours passed quickly as she tapped her fingers to a country gospel station and spun the dial, sampling talk shows. When she arrived in Fargo, North

Dakota, the kids began to wake up. But not Bob. *Wow, he's tired,* thought Audrey. Her seven-year-old appeared in the rearview mirror, rubbing his eyes. "Go back to sleep, honey," said his mom.

Suddenly, the peacefulness of the morning was shattered. "Where's Daddy?" one of the kids asked.

"Very funny," said Audrey, adjusting the mirror. "He's back there sleeping...isn't he?"

The children began pushing pillows aside, looking for Daddy. "Nope," said her seven-year-old, "he's not back here."

"Do you think maybe he got raptured?" another child said. "You know, Mom, like you've been talking about when Jesus comes to get us?"

Audrey wasn't laughing. Panic overtook her as she looked for the next exit. Should she turn around and go back? She had no idea where the rest area was. Was it two hours ago? Three?

Calm down, Audrey, she told herself. Then she prayed, *Dear Lord, help me find Bob. And please keep him safe, wherever he is.*

Pulling into a truck stop, she picked up a pay phone and called the police. "Um...I...uh...left my husband in Minnesota," she told the officer. "At...well...at a rest stop."

There was a moment of silence. "Sorry, could you repeat that?"

After a few minutes punctuated by desperation, Audrey was able to convince the man on the other end of the line that this was no joke—that she had left her husband, but not intentionally, although he might be thinking so.

"Tell you what," said the officer. "You hang on. I'll get all the numbers of the rest stops in that area. You don't go anywhere now, ya hear?"

Audrey didn't go anywhere.

After thanking the officer for his help, she started down the list. One number after another. Each phone call was met with surprise, but no success. Almost out of hope, she dialed the last number on the list. "Do you have a guy there who—?"

"Yaw, I shore do," said a thick Norwegian accent.

Moments later, Bob was on the phone. "Honey, I'm so sorry," said

Audrey. "I didn't mean to—" Audrey started to cry. And Bob started to laugh.

Two hours earlier he had climbed out of the van to use the restroom. But when he came back, the van was gone.

"Ha," Bob had said. "Very funny."

He had walked around the service area three times, expecting to find his family grinning around the next corner. But they were nowhere to be found.

"She wouldn't leave me like this," said Bob. "Would she?"

To pass the time, Bob washed people's windshields and prayed that God would speak loudly to his wife, making his absence apparent. He even climbed in with a trucker who needed some spiritual encouragement. "You know," the trucker told Bob, "this time with you was a divine appointment. I really needed this."

"Dear God," prayed Bob, "please, no more divine appointments tonight."

Early the next morning, Bob watched the headlights of a familiar van pull into the rest stop. He stopped cleaning windshields and breathed a huge sigh of relief. It was a return trip for Audrey. But this time she honked the horn loudly, not caring whom she woke up.

"It's the first time I ever left him," she says, laughing now. "Believe me, it will be the last."

"At first I wondered if the rapture *had* taken place," Bob says. "Then it seemed like something out of a horror movie. But I thought, *Well, make the most of it.*"

Audrey learned a few things, too. "That night I realized the importance of casting all my cares on God. They are His, and He is completely trustworthy.... And I learned that it's always a good idea to count bodies before you pull out onto the freeway."

LOOKING AHEAD...

It happens to all of us. Just when life seems to be humming along smoothly, something as simple as a trip to the restroom turns into one little surprise after another.

There's probably no way to avoid such unwanted twists of fate—but we can control our reaction to them. I've found that adversity in married life is easier to handle when I choose to face it with a smile instead of a frown. So the next time your spouse leaves you stranded by mistake, remember Bob Meisner. You can stew for hours sitting on the curb—or get up and wash a few windshields.

JCD

TWO HUNDRED LAUGHS

A cheerful heart is good medicine,
but a crushed spirit dries up the bones.
Proverbs 17:22

*J*t's been said that the average child laughs two hundred times a day, while the typical adult laughs only four times every twenty-four hours. So what has happened to us grown-ups? Maybe it has something to do with those grueling hours at the office, long lines at the grocery store, and piles of bills on the kitchen counter.

Of course, life can be very difficult, and some people face serious obstacles and hardships. But many of us frown or complain over relatively minor inconveniences. I (JCD) knew a woman who made herself and her husband miserable just because she had one more child than she had bedrooms in which to put them. Too many irritations come from a complete inability to appreciate the humor and blessings that exist around us. When your husband forgets to take the kids to their dentist appointment, or your wife accidentally gives away your favorite sweatshirt, or your toddler draws his version of the Mona Lisa on the living room wall—wouldn't it be easier on everyone if you looked on the funny side of the situation?

Kevin Jones, dealing with increasing paralysis from Lou Gehrig's disease, was asked to describe the worst thing about his condition. He replied, "My wife's driving! She has to take me everywhere."

No matter what you're facing, a smile can only make it better.

Just between us...

- How often do you laugh each day?
- Do we keep our heavenly destination in mind when adversity strikes?
- How could we add humor to the next difficult situation we face?

Dear God, when problems threaten to affect how we treat each other, help us to see them in the perspective of Your unfailing goodness. Amen.

FAMILY WHISPERS

Be joyful always.
1 Thessalonians 5:16

*L*evity and lightheartedness are glue that holds family members together. Families willing to laugh at funny stories about growing up are sure to forge a strong bond for the tough times.

We heard about a mother who decided to hold her squirming toddler in her lap during his first Muppet movie. Midway through, they lost control of a large Pepsi and a box of buttered popcorn. The gooey mixture flowed over the child into the mother's lap. Since the movie was almost over, she decided to sit it out. What she didn't know was that she and her son were being cemented together. When the movie ended, they stood up…and the mother's wraparound skirt stuck to the bottom of the toddler, came unraveled, and followed him up the aisle. She stood there clutching her slip and thanking the Lord she had taken time to put one on!

Another mother wrote us about a little miscommunication involving her preschooler: "Perhaps there should be a uniform word for 'potty' when children have to go to the bathroom. My three-year-old has been taught to refer to that act as a 'whisper.' Well, his grandfather came to visit us, and in the middle of the night my son came to his bed and said, 'Grandpa, I have to whisper.' Not wanting to awaken his wife, he said, 'Okay. Whisper in my ear.'" So the little boy did.

The telling and retelling of funny moments like these can connect families for generations. God created us with a sense of humor for a reason. We believe that He wants us to use it.

Just between us…

- Why do you think that God created us with an ability to laugh?
- Do you remember any funny family stories from your childhood?
- How can we preserve our family heritage through stories?

Lord, we're grateful we can share funny times with our kids. Help us make them part of a grand story that will bind us together for years. Amen.

TUMMY TICKLERS

The cheerful heart has a continual feast.

Proverbs 15:15

*F*or those dismal days when you're in desperate need of a laugh, you might start a humor file filled with surefire tummy ticklers. Here are a few to get you started, all reported to be genuine entries from church bulletins:

—Ushers will eat latecomers.

—The third verse of "Blessed Assurance" will be sung without musical accomplishment.

—Tonight's sermon: "What Is Hell?" Come early and listen to our choir practice.

—Barbara remains in the hospital. She is having trouble sleeping and requests tapes of Pastor Jack's sermons.

—The choir will meet at the Larsen house for fun and sinning.

—The sermon this morning: "Jesus Walks on Water." The sermon tonight: "Searching for Jesus."

—Next Thursday will be tryouts for the choir. They need all the help they can get.

—The cost for attending the Fasting Prayer conference includes meals.

—Ladies, don't forget the rummage sale. It is a good chance to get rid of things not worth keeping around the house. Bring your husbands!

Just between us...

- What is your favorite joke or funny family story?
- Would those with whom we share Jesus Christ describe us as good-humored or somber? How would our children describe us?
- Is there a lot of laughter in our home?

Heavenly Father, we know that a cheerful heart is a blessing to ourselves and others and a response of genuine trust in You. We ask that Your joy bubble up in our daily lives. Amen.

HEALTHY HUMOR

I will watch my ways and keep my tongue from sin.

Psalm 39:1

Laughter is healthy for families. We ought to be able to joke with each other without having to worry about getting an angry overreaction in response. But some humor can be destructive. If your partner is sensitive in a certain area—weight, appearance, intelligence, a specific skill—avoid poking fun at that tender spot. If your child has an embarrassing characteristic, such as bed-wetting or thumb-sucking or stuttering, tread softly. Never ridicule.

We should also note that humor can be a classic response to feelings of low self-esteem. Many of today's most successful comedians got their training while growing up, when they used humor as a defense against childhood hurts. If you're married to someone who'll do anything for a laugh, you may discover that just under the surface he or she is plagued by painful memories or self-doubt.

It's great to laugh—but it's also wise and loving to occasionally check what motivates your humor, where it's aimed, and how it's received. If the person you're having fun with isn't having fun, then it's not real fun at all.

Just between us...

- Have I ever teased you in a way that hurt you? Do we need to apologize for any of our past comments to each other?
- Does either of us use humor to cover up feelings of inferiority?
- Do you think the Lord would approve of the way we use humor? If not, how can we be more careful?

Lord Jesus, You were "a man of sorrows," but You also brought joy to others. We want to always be helpful, never hurtful, in how we express humor in our home. Help us keep our hearts light, our tongues in check, and our motives pure. Amen.

A Lighthearted Spirit

May the God of hope fill you with joy and peace
as you trust in him, so that you may overflow with hope
by the power of the Holy Spirit.
Romans 15:13

*A*s Christians who want to bring joy to our marriages, we might do well to remember the words of baseball great (and occasional comedian) Yogi Berra: "Ninety percent of the game is half mental." We could say the same about life: It's how we look at circumstances that makes all the difference.

For Christians, it's not just how we look at things; it's at Whom we're looking. "Rejoice in the Lord and be glad," wrote David (Psalm 32:11). Paul gave the same advice to the Philippians. And the author of Hebrews wrote: "Let us fix our eyes on Jesus, the author and perfecter of our faith, who for the joy set before him endured the cross...." (Hebrews 12:2). Couples who keep Jesus Christ as Lord of their home seem to laugh more often and cultivate hope in their marriages more easily. Why? Because when Jesus carries the weight of your worries, your needs, and your future, lighthearted living is the natural result.

God gave us a sense of humor to help us stay "half mental" in our marriage, and surely He wants us to use and enjoy it!

Just between us...

- Do you think Jesus often laughed?
- Do you think we would laugh more if we trusted God more?
- What steps can we take to bring a lighthearted spirit into our home?
- How can we worship God by our attitudes about life's little hassles?

Most amazing God, thank You for making humor possible in our world. Forgive us when selfishness, fear, or faithlessness rob us of laughter. Amen.

TOMATO JUICE WARS

Our mouths were filled with laughter,
our tongues with songs of joy.
Psalm 126:2

O ne of the things that first drew me to Jim was his wonderful sense of humor. Even on our first few dates back in 1957, he made me laugh more than any guy I had dated. I loved that about him. He had a clever way of seeing the world around him, and his graphic descriptions were legendary at Pasadena College, where we met. After all these years, we still love to laugh together.

Once when we were flying home from a conference, the flight attendant set a glass of tomato juice on the armrest between us. We both forgot it was there, and Jim knocked it off on my side. About half of the contents landed in my lap.

For some reason, Jim thought that was funnier than I did. While he was laughing with his eyes shut, I poured the other half of the tomato juice in *his* lap. He was still chuckling when the cold juice soaked through to his skin. Then the shock hit him, and the two of us laughed until we had tears in our eyes. It was very difficult to explain what had happened when friends met us at the airport. We looked as though we had attacked each other with chainsaws!

We don't do wild things like that every day, but we try to take advantage of every opportunity to enjoy life. I know that it has helped us cope with the pressures we've experienced along the way. It will help you and your marriage, too.

SMD

Hold on
to Hope

THE GIRL WITH THE APPLE

by Herman and Roma Rosenblat

*I*t is bitter cold on this dark, winter day in 1944. But it is no different than any other day in the Nazi concentration camp. Back and forth I pace, trying to keep my emaciated body warm. I am just a boy, and hungry. I have been hungry for longer than I want to remember. Edible food seems like a dream. Each day, as more of us disappear, the happy past seems also like a dream, and I sink deeper into despair.

Suddenly, I see something moving in the field beyond the camp's two barbed wire fences. Families are working in the field; near the outer fence is a young girl. With an eye out for the guards, I hurry to the inside fence.

The girl stops working and looks at me with sad eyes—eyes that seem to say she understands. I ask, across twenty feet and two fences, if she has something to eat. She reaches into her pocket and pulls out a red apple. A beautiful, shiny red apple. She looks to the left and to the right and then with a smile of triumph, throws the apple over the fences. I pick it up, holding it in trembling, frozen fingers, then run away as fast as I can. If the guards see us, we will both be shot.

The next day, I cannot help myself—I am drawn at the same time to that spot near the fences. Am I crazy for hoping she will come again? Of course. But in here, I cling to any tiny scrap of hope.

She comes. And again, she brings an apple, flinging it over the fences with that same sweet smile. This time I catch it and hold it up for her to see. Her eyes twinkle. And for the first time in so long, I feel my heart move with emotion.

For seven months we meet like this. Sometimes we exchange a few words. Sometimes, just an apple. But she is feeding more than my belly, this angel from heaven. She is feeding my soul. And somehow, I know I am feeding hers as well.

One day I hear frightening news: We are being shipped to another camp. The next day when I greet her, my heart is breaking. I can barely speak. "Do not bring me an apple tomorrow," I say. "I am being sent to another camp. We will never see each other again." Turning before I lose all control, I run away. I cannot bear to look back. If I did, I know she would see tears streaming down my face.

Months pass, and the nightmare continues. Only the memory of this girl sustains me. And then one day, just like that, the nightmare is over. The war has ended. Those of us still alive are freed. I have lost everything precious to me, including my family. But I still have the memory of this girl, a memory I carry in my heart as I move to America to start a new life.

The years go by. It is 1957. I live in New York City. A friend convinces me to go on a blind date with a lady friend of his. Reluctantly, I agree. But she is nice, this woman named Roma. And like me, she is an immigrant, so we have at least that in common.

"Where were you during the war?" Roma asks me gently, in that delicate way immigrants ask one another such questions.

"I was in a concentration camp in Germany," I reply.

Roma gets a faraway look in her eyes.

"What is it?" I ask.

"I am just thinking about something from my past, Herman," Roma explains in a voice suddenly very soft. "You see, when I was a young girl, I lived near a concentration camp. There was a boy there, a prisoner, and for a long while, I used to visit him every day. I remember I used to bring him apples. I would throw the apple over the fence, and he would be so happy."

Roma sighs heavily and continues. "It is hard to describe how we felt about each other—after all, we were so young, and we only exchanged a few words when we could—but I can tell you, there was much love there. I assume he was killed like so many others. But I cannot bear to think that, and so I try to remember him as he was for those months we were given together."

With my heart pounding so hard I think it will explode, I look directly at Roma and ask, "And did that boy say to you one day, 'Do not bring me an apple tomorrow. I am being sent to another camp'?"

"Why, yes," Roma responds, her voice trembling. "But Herman, how on earth could you possibly know that?"

I take her hands in mine and answer, "Because I was that young boy, Roma."

For many moments, there is only silence. We cannot take our eyes from each other as we recognize the soul behind the eyes, the dear friend we once loved so much, whom we have never stopped loving.

Finally, I speak: "Roma, I was separated from you once, and I don't ever want to be separated from you again. Now I am free, and I want to be together with you forever. Dear, will you marry me?"

I see that same twinkle in her eye I used to see as Roma says, "Yes, I will marry you." We embrace—the embrace we longed to share for so many months, but barbed wire came between us. Now, nothing ever will again.

LOOKING AHEAD...

The story you've just read seems too coincidental to be true, but we have verified the account and found that it actually happened. Herman and Roma are still together, and happily married, after all these years. Through published accounts and in their occasional appearances on television, their story—a tale of hope in the midst of terror—has lifted the hearts of thousands.

Can any of us live without hope? I think not. Without hope, we have no reason to get out of bed in the morning…no motivation to complete our daily tasks at work, home, church…no desire to take on the sometimes dizzying array of problems in our world. A life without hope is a life without meaning.

Yet as Christians, we always have hope. In Jesus Christ, we have a holy protector, friend, confidante, and guide. We have a reserved seat in heaven that promises unimaginable joy. This is what gives us the endurance, patience, and motivation to bring glory to our Creator during this imperfect existence. In the days ahead, we'll talk more about how hope can strengthen our marriage.

John tells us, "Whoever believes in the Son has eternal life" (John 3:36). Can you imagine a greater source of hope?

JCD

THE WORLD'S MOST OPPOSITE COUPLE

"We must obey God rather than men!"

Acts 5:29

*A*uthors and counselors Chuck and Barb Snyder describe themselves as the "World's Most Opposite Couple"—and it may be true. Chuck says the only things they have in common are the same wedding anniversary and the same children. He's driven; she's laid-back. She enjoys soft classical music; he prefers country western at maximum volume. She's left-handed; he's right-handed.

And so it goes. Perhaps in part because of their differences, the Snyders have experienced nearly every imaginable conflict in marriage—over scheduling, communication, home life, finances, discipline of the children, and more. In over forty years of marriage, however, the Snyders have learned to appreciate their differences. They have faced, and weathered, more than their share of storms. The key, Chuck says, is nothing fancy—simply obedience to the Lord.

If there's hope for the World's Most Opposite Couple, there's hope for the rest of us, too.

Just between us...

- Were you attracted by my "opposite" traits when we were dating?
- Have we survived despite our differences, or because of them?
- Do we accept the uniqueness of each other as God designed us, or do we struggle to "redesign" each other in our own images?
- Which of my traits that are different from yours do you appreciate most?

Heavenly Lord, thank You for the differences that You weave together to make our marriage strong. Help us to respect, appreciate, and affirm these unique qualities more each day. Amen.

TRANQUILITY

"Be at peace with each other."

Mark 9:50

*I*f you don't protect yourselves from outside stresses, married life can seem more like a marathon than a stroll in the park. With relentless pressure at work, a demanding schedule of carpooling and sports, and the stress of keeping up with home and church duties, moms and dads can begin to lose heart. Then fatigue and irritability set in, angry words are spoken, and soon every member of the family is at one another's throats.

All of us, especially at the end of pressure-packed days, need a safe retreat. As a working husband or wife, you need a chance to unwind privately for a while when you first come home. School kids (teenagers, too) need uninterrupted "down time" on a regular basis. No one can keep up a frenetic schedule for long without it affecting his or her attitude.

Jesus told His followers to "be at peace with each other." If you're finding hopefulness in short supply in your marriage, maybe it's time you get off the treadmill of continuous stress. If it's just the expectations of others that is keeping you on the run, say "no" more often. Take an afternoon off. Get a babysitter so you can have some time to yourself. Set aside quiet time regularly—and guard it. Slow down your mealtimes together. Simplify.

As you make a priority of creating tranquility at home, you'll feel your heart lifting and hope returning.

Just between us...

* When you feel overwhelmed by demands, do you ever lose hope?
* How can we do a better job of protecting each other's "down time"?
* How can tranquility at home promote a better spiritual life?

Dear God, forgive us when we allow external demands to dictate the quality of our home life. Give us the foresight and discipline to create a sanctuary of peace and renewal. Amen.

HEALTHY HOPE

Faith is being sure of what we hope for.
Hebrews 11:1

ope based on the realistic expectation that something can or will change is a powerful, positive, driving force. It motivates us to do our best and helps us achieve what may seem impossible to others. But naive hope that's grounded in wishful thinking can be deeply disappointing and even destructive.

I (JCD) know a woman—I'll call her Martha—who was hurt repeatedly by her father's lack of interest in her. As long as Martha continued to hope he would change, she suffered a fresh wound whenever he missed an important family event or failed to consider her feelings. I urged Martha to realize that her father was emotionally blind—he was incapable of seeing her needs. Once she began to accept his "handicap" as permanent, her pain lessened considerably.

Your partner's temperament or experiences may prevent him or her from fully comprehending your feelings and frustrations. My advice is that you change what can be altered, explain what can be understood, teach what can be learned, revise what can be improved, resolve what can be settled, and negotiate what is open to compromise. Then determine to accept the rest. As you overlook these few "unresolvables" in your relationship, you'll develop a perspective that brings realistic hope for an honest and satisfying marriage.

Just between us...

- What kinds of changes do we hope to see in each other? Are our hopes realistic?
- Would it help our relationship to accept our "unresolvables"?
- What in our marriage gives you the greatest sense of hope?

Father, thank You that You are "the God of all hope." Tonight we look to You for help in bringing honest, healing hope to our marriage. Show us what we can change, show us what we should accept, and bless us with hope. Amen.

ANCHOR FOR THE SOUL

In him our hearts rejoice,
for we trust in his holy name.
Psalm 33:21

When a sudden storm strikes a ship at anchor, only the links of chain and the anchor wedged in the rocks keep vessel and crew from being set dangerously adrift. Obviously, the more tumultuous the times, the more important the moorings. In our own stressful moments, our hopes need to be anchored securely—not in wishes or feelings, but in God's promise. As the author of Hebrews said, "We have this hope as an anchor for the soul, firm and secure" (Hebrews 6:19).

Isn't it comforting to know that we have a secure anchor in our marriages? When storms threaten to overtake us, Jesus Christ will not let us drown. We can count on Him to deliver what He has promised. We may not know what the future holds for our family, career, finances, or dreams—but we can rest in the knowledge that our souls are safe in the hands of almighty God.

Just between us...

- Can you think of a time when you thought the storms of life would capsize you? What kept you afloat?
- Besides God, who or what provides security and stability in your life?
- Do you ever feel adrift spiritually? If so, how can I help?
- Have we placed our hopes and dreams firmly in God's hands? If not, can we do that together now?

Lord, You know the desires of our hearts; You know our secret fears, too. But we acknowledge Your unfailing promises and steadfast love. Thank You for being our rock. Tonight we cast our hopes and dreams on You for safekeeping, because we trust You. Amen.

THE AFTERLIFE

We rejoice in the hope of the glory of God.
Romans 5:2

O ur hope for the afterlife was once expressed to me (JCD) by my father. We were walking on a country road, talking about life and its meaning, when he made a comment that I will never forget. He said that when he was a young man, the possibility of a future heavenly existence was not a matter of great value to him. He had enjoyed his youth, and the thought of life beyond the grave was like a pearl that was crusted over with scales and grime. The beauty of the pearl was assumed, but not apparent or realized. But as he grew older and began to experience problems associated with aging, including a serious heart attack and assorted aches and pains, the beauty of the pearl of eternal life began to shine. It shone more and more brilliantly until it became the most prized of any of his possessions.

My father died shortly after that conversation. He has at last grasped the "pearl" of eternal life. Thankfully, that same blessed hope is available to all of God's children, including you and me. And it is a hope that can bring grace and meaning to every word and activity in our marriage.

Just between us...

- How do you picture heaven?
- As the years pass, do you find yourself thinking more about eternity, or less?
- What is your greatest hope for the future?
- Do we understand that the only "thing" we can take with us to heaven is other people and the Word of God? Do we live as though we believed that?

Father, we are so thankful that You have prepared a place for us in Your kingdom. Help us to make the most of our time in this life. May we do everything in our power to spread the good news of this eternal hope to those who don't know You. Amen.

WORDS OF HOPE

In his word I put my hope.
Psalm 130:5

Like anyone else, I have days when discouragement seems to get the better of me. At such times I try to remember that the Lord has provided me with a source of continuing inspiration and hope. To tap into that source I need simply to open the pages of my Bible, God's letter of hope to me.

I'm reminded of a story about an elderly woman who had lost her husband, George, some years earlier in an automobile accident. Theirs had been a long and happy marriage, and she missed him terribly. When she suffered a broken leg, she felt more confined and alone than ever. One particularly blue day, she found herself longing once again for her husband's company. She sat in her living room and began to weep. "Dear God," she prayed, "please give me the strength to get through this hour."

Get your Bible, a quiet voice inside her said. But her Bible was in the bedroom, and, with her leg in a cast, she thought it would be too hard to retrieve. Then she remembered a small travel Bible on a nearby bookshelf. She reached for it and turned the pages to find a favorite Scripture.

Suddenly a letter fell into her lap. She carefully unfolded the yellowed pages. It was a love letter from George. In it, he expressed his deep affection for her. His words of comfort went straight to her lonely heart.

In the back pages of the Bible she found more notes from George. He had written them in the hospital while awaiting an operation, apparently fearing he would not return home. After he recovered, the notes were forgotten.

That woman spent the rest of the afternoon basking in the company of her husband's letters and in the certainty that the Lord cared for her.

When you're feeling short on hope in your marriage, ask yourself if you've spent enough time lately reading your "mail" from God. Jeremiah wrote, "When your words came, I ate them; they were my joy and my heart's delight" (Jeremiah 15:16). As we go about our days, we can draw on the same delight...if we'll just read the Bible for a few minutes and wait for His Word to meet our need.

God loves you with infinite compassion and tenderness. He knows just what you need and when you need it. In the pages of Scripture, you'll find example after example of His wisdom, comfort, and love—all meant for you. It's the kind of "mail" that will really make your day!

SMD

Dare to Grow

Cool Blades

by Pam Gross

It was a vaguely familiar feeling—a feeling of freedom experienced a lifetime ago. Motion. Speed. Wind. Excitement. Small but present danger. Oh, yes! That same exhilaration that comes with competence. I was doing it!

I was rollerblading on the boardwalk at Seaside, Oregon, on a glorious late summer afternoon. Two miles of flat, smooth pavement, sunshine, ocean air. I couldn't help my smile; it was as ridiculously relentless as a yellow happy face. My body moved with relative ease and a modicum of grace. Push, glide, push, glide—don't lift the feet so high. Swing the hips. Oops! Too much push means too much glide. Let's get more control here. Up and down! Up and down! Miles and miles—every once in a while picking up the scent of a cigar as I once again whizzed past my husband reading Tom Clancy on a bench.

Getting tired, I informed my husband that on the next pass I wanted to stop.

"Okay," he said. "I'll be ready."

Stopping was not a skill I had mastered at that point. As I approached him, I slowed to a more manageable speed. He stood up, swung his arms wide, and enfolded me in a great hug.

"I am your stopping post," he whispered.

I thought, *Yes. What a wonderful metaphor. You are my safe stopping place.*

I sat for a while on the bench enjoying the moment. Some teenagers sauntered past, talking quietly among themselves. The last, a young man of about thirteen, looked admiringly at my skates, bent down, and murmured just so we could hear, "Cool blades." Then he picked up his pace to catch his friends. My husband and I said in unison, "Cool blades?" And we laughed.

Then the sunset zealots began converging like football fans on Super

Bowl Sunday. I hoisted myself off the bench to make the most of the fading light. Up and down, push and glide. Lost in the exquisite rhythm and the elegant air, I almost missed them. But out of the corner of my eye I glimpsed a bicycle surrey pulled up close to the boardwalk. Four women nested there comfortably in that distinctly female way of companionable silence. I thought they were completely absorbed by the inch-by-inch disappearance of the day, but as I moved past, almost out of earshot, I heard the soft call of support: "You go, girl!" To acknowledge, I signaled a "thumbs up" and continued on.

Now, whenever I put on my skates, I hear the young voice saying, "Cool blades," and I smile. When I think of my husband as a safe stopping place, I smile. When I recall the soft call of support, I smile. I'm sure glad I didn't take seriously those people who predicted, "Rollerblade? You're nearly sixty! You'll kill yourself!"

Kill myself? I'd say I was perfectly *alive* that day on the boardwalk.

LOOKING AHEAD...

The routine of what might be called the safe, predictable life has a way of wearing down wives and husbands. Too many years spent in that same office with the broken air conditioner, mowing that same lawn with the crabgrass that never goes away, scraping the ketchup off those same dishes, and making the same lunches for seemingly ungrateful children can leave married couples bored and restless. What's the solution?

One answer is to open your mind to the possibilities around you. Learn a new skill...study a new subject...take on a new hobby...pursue a new adventure. Think about what you've always wanted to try, then do it. You may even find yourself rollerblading down the boardwalk—and loving it.

JCD

TAKING CHANCES

The righteous are as bold as a lion.

Proverbs 28:1

*R*emember Evel Knievel, the death-defying daredevil who jumped over cars, trucks, and all manner of objects on his motorcycle? Evel may have been a little too ambitious for his own good—he broke a number of bones in the process—but he can teach us something about risk.

When we stretch ourselves beyond our comfort zone, we experience the thrill and confidence that comes from facing a new challenge. In the case of a bored husband or wife, this may mean joining a speaker's group, volunteering to lead a Bible study, going on a backpacking trip, or taking a class. It might also include opening up to your spouse or relating the message of Jesus to a group of nonbelievers. For me (JCD), it was leaving a comfortable position as a professor of pediatrics, where I had a predictable income and the support of a large university. I traded that for a little two-room office and called it "Focus on the Family." Only God knew where that radical decision would lead, but it was the beginning of a ride that has resulted in my words being heard worldwide by two hundred million people every day. It was worth the risk, I would say.

Even if you don't do as well as you'd hoped, you'll still feel a sense of fulfillment from reaching for a dream. Just try not to break any bones.

Just between us...

- What kind of positive risks have we taken in our marriage?
- What risks does the Lord want us to avoid?
- What have you always wanted to do, but haven't yet dared to try?
- In what ways can we take a risk for Jesus Christ?

Heavenly Father, we never want fear or complacency in our marriage. By the strength of Your Spirit, may we reach together for new challenges in faith as long as we live. Amen.

WILLING TO FAIL

Instruct a wise man and he will be wiser still.
Proverbs 9:9

*Y*ou may have heard about a remarkable man who encountered continual disappointment yet wasn't afraid to risk failing again. Between 1831 and 1858 he suffered two business failures, the death of his fiancée, and a mental breakdown. This man also failed in his attempts at public office: He bid unsuccessfully for positions as state legislator, speaker of the state legislature, presidential elector, state land officer, congressional representative, U.S. Senator (twice), and U.S. vice president.

Was he a hopeless loser? History indicates otherwise. In 1860, Abraham Lincoln was elected president of the United States. He led the nation through the dark days of the Civil War, preserved the union, and issued the Emancipation Proclamation. Many historians consider him the greatest of all U.S. presidents.

Successful people such as Abraham Lincoln usually experience failure along the way, but they keep taking risks—and they learn from their mistakes. Are you willing to fail in order to learn and grow?

Just between us...

- David was a great king, yet he fell into sin. What did he learn from his sin? (See Psalm 51.)
- What have you learned from past failures?
- When you fail, do I hold it against you, or do I help you try again?
- How does God want us to respond to failure?

Lord, we ask tonight that You affirm Your work in our lives and that You put Your hand of blessing and safekeeping on all our endeavors. When we try and fail, help us to get up and try again. Amen.

ON TARGET

Get a new heart and a new spirit.
Ezekiel 18:31

aybe you heard the story about the day Lisa finally had enough. Her husband, Greg, loved to shoot. An expert marksman, he traveled widely to compete against other enthusiasts, and occasionally he brought home a trophy. But Lisa had no interest in marksmanship. In fact, she didn't like guns—period. To make matters worse, she missed her husband terribly while he was away pursuing his hobby. One day it dawned on her that their relationship was in trouble. That was the day Lisa finally had enough.

Lisa asked Greg to teach her how to shoot a rifle, then joined him in his travels. Soon she decided to compete at the shooting events.

To Lisa's surprise, she liked firing a rifle. And to her husband's surprise, Lisa was a very good shot. She even started bringing home more trophies than he did. But of the prizes they brought home, one stood out above all the rest: Their marriage seemed reborn. The time they spent together at their newfound common interest helped them develop a closeness that simply hadn't existed before.

Lisa's story is a good reminder that what seems like an obstacle might really be an opportunity. Creative, committed couples discover this secret everyday. Just ask a husband who's learned to love ballroom dancing or a wife who's gotten hooked on fly fishing. That's because the best times always seem to come in pairs.

Just between us...

- When was the last time we tried a new activity together?
- Did you enjoy it? Why or why not?
- Are there activities keeping us apart that we could do together?

Dear God, we ask for fresh determination to explore new interests and activities together. Where our marriage would be strengthened by playing together, help us let go of the old habits and assumptions that keep us apart. Amen.

BREAKING OUT

God did not give us a spirit of timidity,
but a spirit of power, of love and of self-discipline.
2 Timothy 1:7

reaking out of comfortable routines can be beneficial for us, but it isn't always as easy as it sounds. My (JCD's) father, for example, hated automatic transmissions on automobiles because he had learned to drive with stick shifts. I've fallen into similar patterns. Until 1992 I wrote books on yellow pads with pencils. I worked that way for years despite the availability of word processors. The twentieth century was almost over before I decided to join it.

Rigidity and the force of habit can cause us to do things that make no sense. Yet when we stop learning and growing, we fail to reach our potential. To look at it another way, which companies would you say are more successful in today's fast-changing marketplace: those whose motto is "We've always done it this way," or those that continually evaluate their methods and seek improvements?

Some of what succeeds in business also makes sense in marriage. You might ask yourself if any outdated routines and pointless—or even costly—habits are holding you back.

Just between us...

- Am I stuck in any habits that no longer make sense?
- How are those who are unwilling to change like the Pharisees of Scripture? (See Luke 11:37–44.)
- Do you enjoy learning?
- How can I encourage you to get out of old ruts or discard outdated habits?

Lord, we can become so comfortable in our old ways, but comfort can lead to stagnation and retreat. Inspire us by Your Spirit "of power, of love and of self-discipline" to reach for Your creative best. Thank You for the gift of new life we can enjoy together every day. Amen.

GROWING WITH GOD

Like newborn babies, crave pure spiritual milk,
so that by it you may grow up in your salvation.
1 Peter 2:2

Our culture tends to emphasize personal growth at the cost of marriage commitment. Humans are made for a lifelong growth curve, and the best place to experience it is inside a faithful, God-blessed marriage. When the Lord Jesus is the "third person" in our union, we can flourish with a spiritual intimacy and growth unavailable to others. I (JCD) am reminded of a letter a woman wrote to me:

> Dear Dr. Dobson:
>
> My husband recently left me after fifteen years of marriage. We had a great relationship, but something was missing—we had no spiritual bond between us. Please tell young couples that there will always be a void in their lives together without Christ. A good marriage must have its foundation in Him in order to experience lasting love, peace, and joy. I am now growing steadily in my walk with the Lord, but I am alone.

Don't forget to grow with God together. The "pure spiritual milk" Peter writes about is the Word of God. Along with Christian fellowship and prayer, the Bible will feed the deepest hungers of your heart. And you'll find the soul-mate of your dreams—sitting right beside you!

Just between us...

- Do our church experiences nurture our spiritual life?
- Do we have friends who encourage our spiritual growth?
- How can we do a better job of growing together in God's Word?

Lord, give us a hunger for Your Word. May we claim the spiritual growth You promise and the emotional and physical intimacy that can come with it. Amen.

BEAUTIFUL MUSIC

Lean not on your own understanding.

Proverbs 3:5

J can't tell you the number of times, especially during our early years together, that the requirements of being a godly wife and mother have seemed to be completely out of reach for me. Perhaps you face similar feelings tonight. You want to keep growing, trying, getting better, but you're not sure if you can hope for success. If so, I want to share one of my favorite stories with you. It reminds me how the Lord can turn our small, sincere efforts into a masterpiece....

Wishing to encourage her young son's progress on the piano, a mother took her small boy to a Paderewski concert. After they were seated, the mother spotted a friend in the audience and walked down the aisle to greet her. The little boy seized the opportunity to explore the wonders of the concert hall. After wandering a while, he eventually made his way through a door marked "No Admittance."

Then the house lights dimmed. The mother returned to her seat for the beginning of the concert only to discover that her son was missing. Before she could start her search, the curtains parted and the spotlights shone on the impressive Steinway grand piano on stage. There, innocently picking out "Chopsticks," sat her little boy. The mother froze in horror. The audience began to murmur with irritation. Meanwhile backstage, the great piano master overheard the childish playing and the rumblings from the audience. Quickly he donned his jacket and made his entrance. Moving to the piano, he whispered in the boy's ear, "Don't quit. Keep playing!" Then Paderewski leaned over, reached around both sides of the boy, and began to improvise a countermelody to harmonize with the boy's rendition of "Chopsticks."

Music—at once childlike and mellow, simple and profound—filled the auditorium. Everyone sat mesmerized, none more so than the boy's awestruck mother....

Do your efforts to grow and flourish in your marriage feel inadequate, timid, unpromising? You're not in this alone! Remember that the Lord's loving arms are around you. Lean on His strength and guidance. You'll grow in ways you never thought possible and make music together more wonderful than you ever imagined.

Our encouragement to you is simple: "Don't quit. Keep playing!" With the blessing of the Master, your efforts together will become something beautiful and unforgettable.

SMD

Glimpse the Moment

OUR NIGHT OF MAGIC

by Charlotte Carpenter

*A*slow but steady rain came down all that wintry morning and froze where it fell—on the ground, the trees, the buildings. By midafternoon the rain had stopped, and we looked on a crystal world.

We were accustomed to the white hoarfrost of winter, but this was something else—a hard, clear coating of solid ice. Our five children, ages five to sixteen, returned from school exclaiming about how good the sledding would be on the steep hill in our pasture.

They took out at once, but they never reached their destination, for between home and hill lay a gently rolling, treeless meadow. Here they found that their sleds would speed over the ice from fence to fence with only the weight of their bodies to keep them going. What fun they had. When they came home to chores and supper, they were so excited. "Mom and Dad, you've got to come with us down to the pasture tonight," they said. They had never seen ice so slippery that they didn't need a hill for coasting on their sleds.

Why should fortyish parents risk life and limb by going out on a dangerously slick night? They begged until we simply could not refuse them.

Gingerly we made our way to the meadow. Even with rubber footgear, we found it hard to walk. The sleds we pulled kept sliding into the backs of our legs. It was very cold, and my husband, the practical one, carried an armload of wood to build a fire.

We will never forget the unbelievably beautiful sight that met our eyes when we reached the meadow. The moon and stars, shining brilliantly as they do only on clear, cold nights, turned the meadow into a lake of glass. We built our fire at the top of a slight incline. The ice reflected us, and the leaping flames danced on the ice.

Again and again the children and sleds flew over the ground. If two rode together, the sled went faster—so fast the riders could barely turn in time to avoid crashing into the fence. The littlest ones rode back to the starting point, easily pulled by older brothers. We parents envied them— the hardest part for us was walking back after the ride. We left most of the sledding to our children and stayed near the fire, absorbed in the dreamlike magic of the night.

We all felt so good when we started back that we hardly noticed our cold feet and tired bodies.

"Will the ice still be here tomorrow?" one of the children asked.

"Probably not if the sun shines," I answered. And sure enough, by midmorning the ice was gone, leaving only an expanse of brown grass.

To this day, when we're in the meadow, whether it's covered with the luxuriant green of summer or the white snow of winter, we remember the wonder of that night. Despite six other witnesses I harbor a slight doubt that it was real, for the experience seems like something we must have imagined.

My husband and I learned several things that night: to enjoy an interlude of joy when it comes; not to put off our children when they find something wonderful and so unusual that it may never happen again; and not to say, "We're too busy now. It will have to wait." We go with them to see a new calf, a robin on the lawn, a butterfly or bug. We share their excitement over a ballgame, a school play, or graduation. For now we know this: Refuse to take the time, and you will miss something precious to hold in memory. A magical sledding on glass in the starlight may happen only once in a lifetime.

LOOKING AHEAD...

Young children view the world with a unique blend of awe and urgency. Everything, from a rainbow to a chocolate sundae, is new and exciting to them. And everything needs to be experienced *right now!*

We sometimes get impatient with this perspective—yet we could learn from it. For as we plow through our endless list of chores and responsibilities, postponing time with our loved ones, life hurtles by—like a sled in a meadow of ice. Before we know it, we're standing before heaven's gates, wondering how we got there so fast. Don't miss the precious nights of magic on the way.

JCD

NUMBERING OF OUR DAYS

*What is your life? You are a mist that
appears for a little while and then vanishes.*
James 4:14

I (JCD) had invited fellow-believer Pete Maravich to join me and a few others for a pick-up basketball game the day before he was to appear on a *Focus on the Family* broadcast. It was an audacious thing to do. Though retired for nearly eight years, "Pistol Pete" had been one of the NBA's all-time best players. Nevertheless, he joined us, and we scrimmaged for about forty-five minutes.

During our break, I asked Pete how he felt. He answered, "I feel just great." Those were his last words. As I turned away, he fell hard on the court. He died seconds later in my arms, the victim of a congenital malformation of the heart that had never been diagnosed.

Moses wrote this prayer: "Teach us to number our days aright, that we may gain a heart of wisdom" (Psalm 90:12). That is a strange verse at first glance. What does knowing that life is short have to do with wisdom? Everything, in fact. If we retained an eternal perspective, we would surely order our choices by eternal values. Would a husband pursue an adulterous affair? Would a wife belittle her mate for his failings? Would both devote their lives to the pursuit of power and wealth? I think not.

Time is an embezzler, juggling the books at night when no one is looking. So remember to use each day for the Lord as though it could be your last. All too quickly, it will be.

Just between us...

* Do we live each day as if it might be our last? Why or why not?
* What does it mean to "live in light of eternity"?
* How can I encourage you to live for things that really matter?

Father, each day of life is a gift, and we do not know when we will draw our last breath. May we live circumspectly, with eternity always in view. Amen.

OVERCOMMITMENT

*Be very careful, then, how you live—not as unwise
but as wise, making the most of every opportunity.*
Ephesians 5:15

O vercommitment is a marriage killer. When your week is filled with the demands of fifty, sixty, or even seventy hours at the office, the pressures of a new baby, making meals, night classes, housework, church programs, replacing the broken window, the kids' band and football practices, Bible studies, painting the house, caring for your aunt with the broken leg...well, you get the idea. How can a husband and wife seek to communicate with each other when they're too worn out to talk? How can they enjoy praying together when every moment is programmed? How can they enjoy a sexual relationship when they just want to collapse into bed each evening?

A few years ago some friends of ours decided to do something about this dilemma. They sold their house and moved to a less expensive home so they could reduce their hours at work and spend more time with each other and their children. That kind of downward mobility is almost unheard of today. Have they regretted it? Not for a moment.

Just between us...
- Are you satisfied with the amount of time we have for rest, renewal, and relationship building?
- Did we overcommit ourselves in the past week or month? How did that happen? How can we prevent it from happening again?
- What activities most often consume the time we could better spend with each other and with God? Can we give some of them up?

Dear Heavenly Father, we find it so much easier to fill our lives with "doing" instead of "being." Forgive us for our misplaced values and careless living, and show us how to keep our priorities straight. Amen.

CHRISTMAS MEMORIES

I thank my God every time I remember you.

Philippians 1:3

*S*ome of my (JCD's) favorite memories are from the Christmas season. I remember the year my father returned from the bank with twenty crisp, new one-dollar bills. Those were the days when a dollar would buy a meal. He attached a Merry Christmas note to each bill and handed one to the newsboy, the shoeshine man, the postman, and seventeen others. He was simply thanking them for being his friends.

Another memory was made years later when Shirley, the kids, and I flew to Kansas City to spend the holidays with my parents. When I stepped off the plane and into the terminal, I caught sight of my father. He had a twinkle in his eyes and a smile on his face; Mom also was aglow with excitement. Their family had come home. I wouldn't trade those memories for anything.

Every season offers opportunities for unforgettable moments to share with your spouse and family. Seize them—and savor them.

Just between us...

- What is your favorite holiday? Why?
- What is your fondest memory of a holiday season we've spent together?
- What can we do to keep alive the memory of all our special moments?
- How can we make our faith a more central part of our family celebrations?

Lord, thank You for giving us "the heritage of those who fear Your name." Thank You for the many special times You have given us and for the wonderful memories that go with them. May we recognize and cherish these gifts and pass them on to our children. Amen.

EVERYDAY MOMENTS

I was filled with delight day after day.
Proverbs 8:30

We all cherish the milestones and special events in the course of married life: the wedding and honeymoon, the birth of children, the twenty-fifth and fiftieth wedding anniversaries, the kids' high school and college graduations. These are occasions to celebrate with hugs, photographs, and congratulations all around. But don't forget to savor the everyday moments that make up the rest of our days. Think about what it means to wake up in the morning next to someone you love and to begin the day with a kiss…to exchange knowing glances with your partner as you rake leaves in the yard or share a cup of coffee…to hold hands with your mate in church as you sing praises to our glorious God.

When you review the mental scrapbook of images from your marriage, we hope it is filled with happy memories of the "big moments" you've shared together. But also be sure to include snapshots of those joyful, everyday events that make each day of marriage something special.

Just between us…

- What everyday activities bring you joy?
- Do you think we have lived from one big event to the next—or have we tried to make ordinary days special, too?
- How can we help each other savor everyday moments?
- Do our lives demonstrate to others that each moment is a gift from God?

Father, we find Your love in the simple joys around us—a bird's song or a smile from our mate, blue skies or the laughter of children. Thank You for health and for Your unfailing abundance. Open our eyes to the wealth of each day, O Lord. May we never live like paupers when You have made us so rich. Amen.

LAST CALL

The great day of the LORD is near—
near and coming quickly.
Zephaniah 1:14

*T*hink about the people you love. Have you thanked them recently for what they mean to you? If the Lord called you home this evening, would you feel satisfied that you had told them everything you needed to say?

In the last months of my (JCD) mother's life, she had end-stage Parkinson's disease and was unable to communicate or understand us. One day, however, the Lord granted us a reprieve. When Shirley and I visited the nursing home, my mother instantly recognized us, and I was able to thank her for being a good mother, for staying true to Jesus, and for sacrificing to put me through college. She smiled; she understood. I told her that my father was waiting for her in heaven and that Jesus would say, "Well done! Thou good and faithful servant." I prayed for her and thanked the Lord for her love in my life. She returned our love, and we said good-bye.

That was the last rational conversation I had with my mother, and I will always be thankful for those final moments together. In this temporary existence, we must always seize opportunities to communicate soul to soul. Cherish each moment with your partner, family, and friends. Tell them how important they are to you. Above all, live each day so that when the final call comes, Jesus will say, "Well done! Thou good and faithful servant."

Just between us...

- Do we tell our loved ones what they mean to us?
- What would you like to say to me "soul to soul"?
- Are we ready for the Lord to call us home? What should we do to prepare?

Dear Lord, thank You for my lifetime partner. May we never miss an oppor-
tunity to say the words that really count. Help us to live without regrets, always
ready for the homeward call of Jesus. Amen.

STILL THE ONE

If we love one another, God lives in us
and his love is made complete in us.
1 John 4:12

e've talked this week about the brevity of life and the importance of making the most of the time the Lord has given us. Our journey as marital partners will someday come to an end. First one of us, and then the other, will stand before God, give an account of our days, and begin our eternal journey.

Jim and I certainly look forward to that heavenly reward, but we are also enjoying our time together on this earth. Jim has recovered fully from a heart attack and a stroke, either of which could have taken his life. Those experiences have made our relationship all the sweeter and more precious. I will always thank God for bringing us together in a marriage that has continued now for more than four decades.

One of the most delightful experiences during that time came in a Marriage Encounter seminar we participated in years ago. I knew that Jim loved and needed me during the early years of our marriage, but I had begun to quietly wonder if I *still* held the most prominent place in his heart. On the final day of the seminar, without discussing it ahead of time, we wrote each other letters addressing just this issue. I'll never forget the moment we came together and shared these thoughts.

Jim concluded his letter to me, in part, with these words:

I love you, S. M. D. (Remember the monogrammed shirt?) I love the girl who believed in me before I believed in myself. I love the girl who never complained about huge school bills and books and hot apartments and rented junky furniture and no vacations and humble little Volkswagens. You have been *with* me—encouraging me, loving me, and supporting me since August 27, 1960. And the status you have given me in our home is beyond what I have deserved.

So why do I want to go on living? It's because I have you to take the journey with. Otherwise, why make the trip? The half that lies ahead promises to be tougher than the years behind us. Autumn is coming. Even now, I can feel a little nip in the air—and I try not to look at a distant, lone cloud that passes near the horizon. With whom, then, will I spend that final season of my life?

None but you, Shirls. The only joy of the future will be in experiencing it as I have the past twenty-one years—hand-in-hand with the one I love, a young miss named Shirley Deere, who gave me everything she had—including her heart. Thank you, babe, for making this journey with me. Let's finish it—together!

May the Lord continually sustain and enrich your marriage. God's blessings to you both…and good night.

SMD

Epilogue

We hope that the words in this book have in some way inspired or encouraged you as you seek to strengthen your marriage. May the rest of your years together be full of joy and a deepening appreciation for each other.

In many ways, marriage is like a marathon. To succeed at it, a husband and wife must be disciplined and committed. But that may not be enough. Only when you both turn to Jesus Christ will you find the love, courage, and answers you need to keep going right on to the finish line. As you apply the biblical principles in this book, you will be better prepared to make the words of the apostle Paul the autobiography of your marriage: "I have fought the good fight, I have finished the race, I have kept the faith" (2 Timothy 4:7).

Marriage is a wonderful gift from God—and so is your mate. Enjoy each day of your journey together! We both will be waiting for you one day at the finish line called eternity.

Jim and Shirley Dobson

INTRODUCTION
Marriage study conclusion from David Popenoe and Barbara Dafoe Whitehead, "The State of Our Unions: The Social Health of Marriage in America," The National Marriage Project, Rutgers University, 1999.

WEEK ONE
Sunday: "SHMILY" by Laura Jeanne Allen. © 1997. Used by permission of the author.

Tuesday: Illustration from *Jumping Hurdles, Hitting Glitches, Overcoming Setbacks* by Steve Brown (Colorado Springs, Colo.: NavPress Publishing Group, 1992).

Saturday: Illustration by Debbi Smoot from *Moments for Each Other* by Robert Strand (Green Forest, Ariz.: New Leaf Press, 1993). Reprinted in *More Stories for the Heart*, comp. Alice Gray (Sisters, Ore.: Multnomah Publishers, Inc. 1997).

WEEK TWO
Sunday: "I'm Third," retold by James Lund. This story originally appeared in the *Denver Post* in the late 1950s.

Thursday: Survey result from *Love for a Lifetime* by Dr. James Dobson (Sisters, Ore.: Multnomah Publishers, Inc., 1998).

WEEK THREE
Sunday: "Protected by Prayer" by Cheri Fuller. Taken from *When Families Pray* by Cheri Fuller. © 1999. Used by permission of Multnomah Publishers, Inc.

WEEK FOUR
Sunday: "Do You Want Me?" by Park York. Taken from the June 1989 issue of the *Christian Herald*. Reprinted by permission of the *Christian Herald*.

WEEK FIVE
Sunday: "Men Have a Six-Word Limit" by Erma Bombeck, from *Forever, Erma* © 1996 by the Estate of Erma Bombeck. Reprinted with permission of Andrews and McMeel Publishing. All rights reserved.

Wednesday: "Quick Listening," in *Incompatibility: Still Grounds for a Great Marriage* by Chuck and Barb Snyder (Sisters, Ore.: Multnomah Publishers, Inc. 1999).

Thursday: Word picture illustration from *The Language of Love* by Gary Smalley and John Trent (Pomona, Calif.: Focus on the Family Publishing, 1988).

WEEK SIX
Sunday: "Head of the House" by Thom Hunter. Taken from *Those Not-So-Still Small Voices* (NavPress). © 1993. Used by permission of the author.

Tuesday: Tendencies of the single man from *Sexual Suicide* by George Gilder (New York, N.Y.: Quadrangle/The New York Times Book Company, 1973).

Friday: Quotation from *From Ashes to Glory* by Bill McCartney (Nashville, Tenn.: Thomas Nelson, Inc., Publishers, 1995).

WEEK SEVEN
Sunday: "Martha's Secret Ingredient" by Roy J. Reiman, courtesy of *Reminisce* magazine. Used by permission.
Friday: Camping illustration from *Hidden Keys of a Loving, Lasting Marriage* by Gary Smalley (Grand Rapids, Mich.: Zondervan Publishing House, 1984, 1988).

WEEK EIGHT
Sunday: "That's the Way I Feel about You" by Nancy Jo Sullivan. Taken from *Moments of Grace* by Nancy Jo Sullivan. © 2000. Used by permission of Multnomah Publishers, Inc.

WEEK NINE
Sunday: "Romance" by Bill and Lynne Hybels. Taken from *Fit to Be Tied* by Bill and Lynne Hybels. © 1991 by Bill and Lynne Hybels. Used by permission of Zondervan Publishing House.

WEEK TEN
Sunday: "A Gentle Caress" by Daphna Renan. Used by permission of the author. Daphna Renan is a graduate of Yale College. She has published several short stories in several anthologies. She can be contacted by e-mail at daphna.renan@yale.edu.
Monday: Sexual motives from *What Wives Wish Their Husbands Knew about Women* by Dr. James Dobson (Wheaton, Ill.: Tyndale House Publishers, 1975).
Wednesday: Twelve Steps from *Intimate Behavior* by Desmond Morris (New York, N.Y.: Random House, 1971).

WEEK ELEVEN
Sunday: "Dream Lover, Where Are Yoo-Oo-Oou?" by Patrick O'Neill. Taken from the Tuesday, October 3, 1989 issue of *The Oregonian*, © 1989, Oregon Publishing Co. All rights reserved. Reprinted with permission.

WEEK TWELVE
Sunday: "Surprise Party" by Gary Smalley. Taken from *Love Is a Decision* by Gary Smalley. © 1992. Word Publishing, Nashville, Tenn. Used by permission. All rights reserved.
Thursday: Illustration from *Building Your Mate's Self-Esteem* by Dennis and Barbara Rainey (San Bernardino, Calif.: Here's Life Publishers, 1986).

WEEK THIRTEEN
Sunday: "May I Have This Dance?" by Nancy Jo Sullivan. Taken from *Moments of Grace* by Nancy Jo Sullivan. © 2000. Used by permission of Multnomah Publishers, Inc.

WEEK FOURTEEN
Sunday: "The Peanut Vendor" by Sam Kameleson. Taken from *The Christ-Centered Marriage*, © 1996 by Neil T. Anderson and Charles Mylander, Gospel Light/Regal Books, Ventura, Calif., 93003. Used by permission.
Monday: Larry Burkett excerpt from *Love for a Lifetime* by Dr. James Dobson (Sisters, Ore.: Multnomah Publishers, Inc. 1998)

WEEK FIFTEEN

Sunday: "A Most Extraordinary Event" by Jo Ann Larsen. © 1992. Used by permission of the author.

Thursday: Illustration from *More of... The Best of Bits and Pieces,* ed. Rob Gilbert (Fairfield, N.J.: The Economics Press, 1997). Reprinted in *Stories for a Man's Heart,* comp. Al and Alice Gray (Sisters, Ore.: Multnomah Publishers, Inc., 1999).

Friday: Illustration by Barbara Johnson from *We Brake for Joy!* by Patsy Clairmont, Barbara Johnson, Marilyn Meberg, Luci Swindoll, Sheila Walsh, and Thelma Wells (Women of Faith, Inc., 1998). Reprinted in *Stories for a Man's Heart,* comp. Al and Alice Gray (Sisters, Ore.: Multnomah Publishers, Inc., 1999).

WEEK SIXTEEN

Sunday: "The Argument" by Gigi Graham Tchividjian. Taken from *Weather of the Heart* by Gigi Graham Tchividjian. ©1993. Used by permission of Baker Book House Company.

WEEK SEVENTEEN

Sunday: "The Face of My Enemy" by Corrie ten Boom. Taken from *The Hiding Place* by Corrie ten Boom with John and Elizabeth Sherrill. Used by permission of Chosen Books LLC, Chappaqua, N.Y.

Monday: "Dear Abby" illustration from *The Christ-Centered Marriage* by Neil T. Anderson and Charles Mylander (Ventura, Calif.: Gospel Light/Regal Books, 1996).

WEEK EIGHTEEN

Sunday: "Johnny Lingo's Eight-Cow Wife" by Patricia McGerr. © 1965 by Patricia McGerr. First published in *Woman's Day*. Reprinted by permission of Curtis Brown, Ltd.

WEEK NINETEEN

Sunday: "Ragamuffin Brother" by Ron Mehl. Taken from *God Works the Night Shift* by Ron Mehl. © 1994. Used by permission of Multnomah Publishers, Inc.

Tuesday: Illustration from *The Signature of Jesus* by Brennan Manning (Sisters, Ore.: Multnomah Books, 1992). Reprinted in *Stories for a Man's Heart,* comp. Al and Alice Gray (Sisters, Ore.: Multnomah Publishers, Inc., 1999).

Wednesday: Language research and comments from "Infants' Memory for Spoken Words" by P. W. Juscyzk and E. A. Hohne (*Science,* 26 September 1997) and "Parents Beware: Little Ears Are Listening" by Rachel Ellis (*Associated Press,* http://www.ap.org/, 26 September 1997).

WEEK TWENTY

Sunday: "Hi There!" by Nancy Dahlberg. Taken from *American Baptist,* December 1981. Used by permission.

Tuesday: Illustration from *Quiet Times with the One You Love* by Art Hunt (Sisters, Ore.: Multnomah Publishers, Inc., 1998).

WEEK TWENTY-ONE

Sunday: "Surprise, Surprise, Surprise!" by Philip Gulley. Taken from *Front Porch Tales* by Philip Gulley. © 1997. Used by permission of Multnomah Publishers, Inc.

Monday: Illustration from *Four Pillars of a Man's Heart* by Stu Weber (Sisters, Ore.: Multnomah Publishers, Inc., 1997).

WEEK TWENTY-TWO

Sunday: "Dear Daddy" by Gary Smalley and John Trent. Taken from *The Language of Love* by Gary Smalley and John Trent, Ph.D., a Focus on the Family book published by Tyndale House. © 1988, 1991 by Gary Smalley and John Trent, Ph.D. All rights reserved. International copyright secured. Used by permission.

Tuesday: Material on divorce from "Children of Divorce Heal Slowly, Study Finds; Scholar's Latest Evidence in Influential Series" by Barbara Vobejda (*Washington Post*, 3 June 1997), and presentation given by Dr. Armand Nicholi at the White House Conference on the State of the American Family, 3 May 1983. Available in the *Congressional Record*, Extension of Remarks, 3 May 1983.

Wednesday: Divorce research material from *Home with a Heart* by Dr. James Dobson (Wheaton, Ill.: Tyndale House Publishers, 1996).

WEEK TWENTY-THREE

Sunday: "What about Bob?" by Phil Callaway. Taken from *Who Put the Skunk in the Trunk?* by Phil Callaway. © 1999. Used by permission of Multnomah Publishers, Inc.

WEEK TWENTY-FOUR

Sunday: "The Girl with the Apple" by Herman and Roma Rosenblat. © 1998. Used by permission of the authors.

Saturday: Illustration by Lucille Heimrich from *A Match Made in Heaven* by Susan Wales and Ann Platz (Sisters, Ore.: Multnomah Publishers, Inc., 1999).

WEEK TWENTY-FIVE

Sunday: "Cool Blades" by Pam Gross. © 1997. Used by permission of the author. Pam Gross is president of CareerMakers, a life planning and career management firm in Portland, Oregon. She is the author of *Want a New, Better, Fantastic Job?* and can be reached at either (503) 297-6689 or pam@careermakers.com.

Saturday: Illustration by Charles Swindoll from *Growing Strong in the Seasons of Life* (Zondervan Publishing House, 1983). Reprinted in *Stories for the Heart*, comp. Alice Gray (Sisters, Ore.: Multnomah Publishers, Inc., 1996).

WEEK TWENTY-SIX

Sunday: "Our Night of Magic" by Charlotte Carpenter. © 1993. Excerpted from *Legacies*, ed. Maury Leibovitz and Linda Solomon, published by HarperCollins. Reprinted with permission.

STRAIGHT TALK TO MEN

In this classic book, Dr. James Dobson shows the difference between the world's perspective and God's perspective on manhood, giving you the information you need to build a strong home.

ISBN 1-59052-356-3

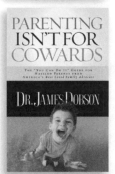

PARENTING ISN'T FOR COWARDS

Let's face it, raising children is often difficult, especially in this shock-wave world. Dr. James Dobson helps parents navigate the passage from early childhood through adolescence.

ISBN 1-59052-372-5

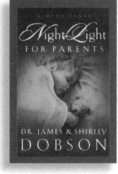

NIGHT LIGHT FOR PARENTS

The Dobsons follow up their original bestselling devotional with another Gold Medallion winner. Discover a daily dose of practical, personal, and spiritual insights for parenting children of all ages.

ISBN 1-57673-928-7

CERTAIN PEACE IN UNCERTAIN TIMES

Fight violence, hunger, disease, and death—on your knees! National Day of Prayer Task Force chairwoman Shirley Dobson shows you how to nurture a true and lasting lifestyle of prayer.

ISBN 1-57673-937-6

BUILD A MARRIAGE THAT WILL GO THE DISTANCE

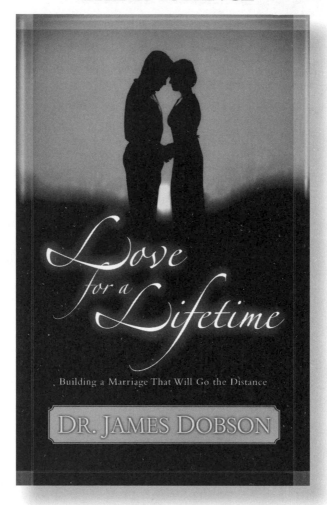

For over ten years, the bestselling Gold Medallion–winner *Love for a Lifetime* has brought hope, harmony, and healing to millions of homes, giving men and women powerful insights for building lasting marital harmony. This book is perfect for every man, woman, or couple who wants to strengthen the foundation and/or celebrate the success of their marriage relationship. And it's ideal for gift-giving—not only to couples celebrating their anniversary, but to newlyweds, married couples, men and women who are engaged, and any husband and wife who want to enhance their marriage. Now this classic has a fresh new cover that will give it even wider appeal.

ISBN 1-57673-770-5